THE
GOSPEL
OF JOHN

THE GOSPEL OF JOHN

In the Light of the Old Testament

CLAUS WESTERMANN

Translated by Siegfried S. Schatzmann

HENDRICKSON
PUBLISHERS

*I dedicate this study to the "Wieslocher group," with
whom I have conducted Bible studies over many
years, including on the Gospel of John. In the course
of working with this group and in preparing for it,
it became clear to me that the Old Testament sheds
light on many still unresolved issues pertaining to
the interpretation of the Gospel of John. My gratitude
belongs to the group for their fine cooperation.*

English translation © 1998 by Hendrickson Publishers, Inc.
P. O. Box 3473, Peabody, Massachusetts 01961–3473
All rights reserved

Printed in the United States of America
ISBN 1–56563–237–0

Original German edition: DAS JOHANNESEVANGELIUM AUS DER SICHT
DES ALTEN TESTAMENTS, ©1994 Calwer Verlag, Stuttgart.

First Printing — April 1998

Library of Congress Cataloging-in-Publication Data

Westermann, Claus.
  [Johannesevangelium aus der Sicht des Alten Testaments. English]
  The Gospel of John in the light of the Old Testament / Claus
Westermann; translated by Siegfried S. Schatzmann.
  Includes bibliographical references and index.
  ISBN 1–56563–237–0 (paper)
  1. Bible. N.T. John—Criticism, interpretation, etc. 2. Bible. N.T.
John—Relation to the Old Testament. 3. Bible. O.T.—Relation to John.
I. Title.
BS2615.2.W46513   1998
226.5′06—dc21   98–14164
                                                                       CIP

Table of Contents

1

Introduction

Assumptions

In the present phase of biblical interpretation, it is no longer possible to conduct Old and New Testament exegesis in isolation from one another. There are areas, of course, in which this continues to be possible, if not indeed called for, but we can no longer rule out the question of their reciprocal relationship. This question is not only posed from the perspective of the Christian tradition, in which the Old and the New Testaments are *one* book. Add to this the new situation in which, on the one hand, Jewish exegesis interprets the writings of the Torah without any regard for the writings of the New Testament and, on the other hand, Christian exegetes frequently understand the New Testament entirely from the vantage point of the Jewish tradition. It is equally significant that advancing secularization means that the books of both the Old and the New Testaments have long been read and interpreted outside the confines of ecclesiastical-religious commitment.

I want to demonstrate from the Gospel of John how close to one another agreement and sharp contrast can be if John's Gospel is read from the perspective of the Old Testament. It becomes evident that there are contexts in which critical questions pertaining to the Old Testament must be addressed to the texts of the New Testament as well.

The Gospel of John is an account. The Old Testament, too, contains many accounts, in differing forms and not just in the historical books. Many of these accounts include God speaking or acting. Accounts of God sending someone with a mission are told in the prophetic books as well as in the Gospel of John. Jesus is sent by God, just as the prophets were God's envoys. Jesus is sent to the same people. He speaks the same language. Those to whom he is sent live and think within the traditions and atmosphere that shape the Old Testament; they live within the history that began with their forefathers. When Jesus took on humanity among humans, he addressed *these* humans and ministered among them. He spoke their language and shared their thinking. Only in this way was he able to gain their confidence. The history of Jesus of Nazareth cannot be understood except against the backdrop of the Old Testament.

The Prologue: John 1:1–18

A considerable amount of gnostic elements is ascribed to the Gospel of John. It certainly does contain gnostic motifs and gnostic terms, as well as gnostic thought. But the example of the prologue illustrates that they are limited to a minor segment:

	Prologue of the Gospel	Gnostic Revision	Additions
1	In the beginning was the Word, and the Word was with God,		
2		and the Word was God. He was in the beginning with God;	
3	all things were made through him, and without him was not anything made that was made.		

4	In him was life, and the life was the light of men.	
5		The light shines in the darkness, and the darkness has not overcome it.	
6–8		John
9		The true light that enlightens every man was coming into the world.	
10	He was in the world, and the world was made through him, yet the world knew him not.	
11	He came to his own home, and his own people received him not.	
12a	But to all who received him,	
12b	he gave power to become children of God;	who believed in his name,	
13		who were born, not of blood nor of the will of the flesh nor of the will of man, but of God.	
14	And the Word became flesh and dwelt among us, full of grace and truth; we have beheld his glory, glory as of the only Son from the Father	
15		John
16	And from his fulness have we all received, grace upon grace.	
17			For the law was given through Moses; grace and truth came through Jesus Christ.
18	No one has ever seen God; the only Son, who is in the bosom of the Father, he has made him known.	

The Compositional Nature of 1:1–18

The account of Jesus of Nazareth begins in 1:19, written in prose. The preceding prologue probably was a *poem*. It is a *prologue* to the extent that it summarizes the Gospel as a whole (except for the passion narrative); this is especially true of vv. 11–12. This formerly independent poem has been reworked subsequently, as the additions of vv. 6–8, 15 (John), and 17 (law) indicate.

Even without these additions, the prologue still is not a smooth text; the rhythm of the poem is disturbed at several points. It has undergone gnostic reworking, as indicated by the gnostic language in the additions. Furthermore, there are awkward repetitions.

Verse 5 represents an addition (light and darkness, anticipating v. 14), as does v. 9 (intensification of the gift of salvation through the word "true"; cf. ch. 6: "the true bread," "that which comes down from heaven"). Together vv. 5 and 9 form one addition (interrupted by vv. 6–8, dealing with John). At the end of the first part (vv. 1–13) there is a further gnostic addition in vv. 12b, 13, which attempts to provide a more specific explanation for the expression "to all" in v. 12a, that is, "to all" who were not born of humanity but of God. The contrast between heavenly and earthly is a recurring one in Gnosticism.

In gnostic thought, the separation into a heavenly and an earthly realm is assumed from the start. Creation and redemption coincide, as the additions in vv. 1–13 demonstrate; this might also explain the otherwise obscure additions about John in 1:6–8, 15: John is to be part even of the beginning.

It is important to add here that the distinction between the prologue and its additions can at best be assumed, because it offers a more plausible understanding of the text. It is not possible to be absolutely certain about this matter. The transmitted text retains its own meaning, all the same. *Without* the additions, it gains the structure indicated above.

1:1–13: The Word in the Beginning

Like the whole Bible, the Gospel of John begins with creation. Genesis 1 presents it as a creation by the Word. From Gen 1 the prologue has taken up the concept that everything in creation was made by the Word. It is the creative Word that has become flesh (human) in Jesus.

The transition from the first to the second part, in vv. 11, 12, speaks of the incarnation of the Word and as such constitutes a brief summary of the Gospel:

"He came to his own home" (— chs. 1–6).
"His own people received him not" (— chs. 7–12).
"To all who received him, . . . he gave power
    to become children of God" (— chs. 13–17:
    farewell discourses).

1:14–18: The Word Became Flesh

The second part (vv. 14–18) begins with the elemental statement, "The Word became flesh and dwelt among us." The event of the Word becoming flesh, the incarnation, is contained within this statement. Encompassing the entire Gospel, this sentence (v. 14a) is followed by a confession in vv. 14b and 16 (v. 15 is a supplement about John)—a joyous confession by those who through Jesus' coming have experienced grace upon grace, an abundance of acts of grace. If the first phrase, "The Word became flesh," is followed by a second one, "and dwelt among us," the latter signifies, with regard to the Old Testament, that it was not merely a momentary vision of God (as, e.g., in Gen 28) but that in his Son, God remained present among people from the beginning to the end of his ministry, as a human among humans, within the boundaries of human existence.

The purpose of the prologue is the confession of those who shared this experience; they are able to speak as eye- and earwitnesses. What they saw they express in the clause "we have beheld his glory." These words can only mean: What we saw was his glory concealed in human form. What they experienced through this is expressed as a glory of the Son of God in the lowliness of his incarnation, which for them meant an abundance of favor, a wealth of salvific acts. This is then addressed in the three parts of the Gospel that were foreshadowed in vv. 11–12.

The final statement, v. 18, sounds like a postscript to the prologue: The Son has made the invisible God known to us. Even though the Old Testament speaks of many theophanies, what has taken place now is unique and amazing: God became human in Jesus and dwelt among people.

Listening to the prologue, one is reminded of the calling of the prophet Isaiah, who in his vision saw God enthroned in his glory but then received a mission and was given a task that he was to carry out in his lowliness, exposed to every hostility without power and without protection. Here, too, the glory of God was concealed in the lowliness in which the one sent from God was to walk. It is this hidden glory to which the Gospel will witness on Jesus' journey and in his ministry, with which God has commissioned him. The disciples found this glory in Jesus' ministry and proclamation.

2

The Components of the Gospel

The Gospel is a literary composition. It assumes a discernible structure that is already indicated in the prologue (1:11–12):

Chs. 1–6:   "He came to his own home."

Chs. 7–12:   "His own people received him not."

Chs. 13–17: "To all who received him, . . . he gave power to become children of God."

Chs. 18–21: Jesus' suffering, death and resurrection.

These parts, however, do not provide a seamless account, as if it had been penned in one sitting. This can be observed in the passion narrative of chs. 18–21, which John's Gospel has in common with the Synoptics.

Chapters 1–6 and 7–12 encompass the period of Jesus' ministry, his acts and discourses. Many elements of these chapters were originally independent, for instance, the healing narratives, which were formed orally, as in the Synoptics, and were initially handed down orally. Hence, in the case of some of the texts, there must have been an *oral phase* preceding them. Chapters 7–12, too, did not come about as a unit but were composed of different elements. Thus, chs. 13–17 are part of Jesus' life and ministry as well, that is, the farewell discourses, for which there is nothing corresponding in the Synoptics.

The Structure of the Narratives in Chapters 1–12

The basic structure of the Gospel is that of a story. The passion narrative is a coherent account, on which the Gospel focuses from the outset. The structure is made up of itineraries and brief reports. The discourses, as well as the acts of Jesus, are integrated into this structure. The prologue, too, has the form of a story.

The travel references.   Jesus ministered as an itinerant. If his ministry was to be recounted contextually, there was no option other than an account of his journeys. In many parts of the world the recounting of a journey was a very early medium for handing down tradition. It plays a significant part in the Old Testament. Descriptions of journeys were not a matter of invention. This also applies to place references, such as John 4:5–6: "Jacob's well was there." These also originated in the oral tradition. The generation following the disciples could learn of Jesus' ministry only on the basis of the places where Jesus had ministered. Particularly helpful are the instances where, along with a location, it is mentioned that Jesus had visited that location and what had happened there.

The accounts.   Individual brief accounts at the beginning form a prehistory: one about John the Baptist (1:19–34; 3:23–36) and another about the call of the first disciples (1:35–51). Important elements are the brief accounts, sometimes only one sentence long.

The accounts about *the effect* of Jesus' words and deeds run through the entire Gospel, up to the beginning of the passion narrative. They all resemble one another. The parallelism of differing responses remains to the end: At no point does no one believe; at no point does everybody believe. The accounts are limited to a restricted context; they address only the ministry and teaching of Jesus. Some approve of it, others argue that he is leading people astray. A division arises over it.

Accounts of actions by Jesus' opponents. An intensification can be observed in these accounts, leading to the passion narrative. Jesus' opponents attempt to seize him. They send temple guards to arrest him (7:32, 45). Repeatedly they intend to stone him. In the end, they decide to put him to death for fear of a tumult (11:47–53). They order that he be reported to them.

These very terse narrative statements are linking segments of an action or a discourse, either introducing or concluding them. Their purpose is to allow the entire account to function as a unified narrative. In this regard, they resemble parts of the book of Jeremiah, in which the words and actions lead to a passion narrative as well. Here, too, the relationship between the story of Jesus of Nazareth and that of the prophet is difficult to miss.

The Acts of Jesus in Chapters 1–12

The Healings

To perceive Jesus' healings merely as isolated acts in his life, or as a sign of something greater, means to misconstrue them. They can be explained only on the basis of their prehistory in the Old Testament, which already relates healings by prophets. Their concern is to reveal the works of God in a suffering individual.

4:46b–54: The official of Capernaum. The prerequisite for the healings was the unconditional trust in the healer. In the case of the official from Capernaum, it was trust from a distance; he had only heard of Jesus (cf. 1 Kgs 5). The narrative indicates that this trust is possible for everyone, that everyone has access to him. It is a personal trust, like that found in the Psalms of trust in the Old Testament, the entrusting of self by the whole person. It is not a form of believing equivalent to a conviction and a viewpoint, such as whether or not Jesus is the Messiah. In the Psalms it denotes the trust into which laments are transformed (Pss 13; 22). It is the work of his Father, whom the suffering ones in the old covenant implored to transform their sorrow. The healings of Jesus are significant because in them the one who transforms sorrow has become human. They can be understood only against the backdrop of the laments of the Old Testament.

5:1–16: At the pool of Bethesda. Just as in the Old Testament journey accounts, the distinctiveness of the location is explained at the outset. Jesus comes this way and attends to *one* sick man; therein lies the distinctiveness of this healing. It is precisely the description of the multitude of the sick who hope for their healing that demonstrates clearly that there is a limit to Jesus' ministry here: Jesus is a human being with limitations. He can attend to only *one* sick man; the prerequisite for this is the personal contact: "Do you want to be healed?" The question can mean only this. That he understands people (4:7ff.) holds also for the healings. Jesus' compassion for the sick man stands in contrast to the rigid legal piety of the Jews, for whom this healing is sin because it occurred on the Sabbath. The response of the one healed is directed against them: "The man who healed me said to me. . . ." Now he obeys the one who healed him.

9:1–41: The healing of a man born blind. The disciples ask a theological question: "Rabbi, who sinned, this man or his parents . . . ?" Jesus answers, "that the works of God might be made manifest in him." The disciples accept this man's blindness as a fact, while Jesus has compassion on the one who suffers. The disciples are locked into the doctrine of recompense, and living with Jesus has evidently not brought about a change in this. By means of his response, Jesus implies that it is not true that for every sickness there has to be some blame. Against this he argues that the works of God are the works of the one who heals; they can be brought to bear upon everyone. As long as there is life in human beings, wonderful things can happen to them. The continuation of the narrative indicates that the reaction to the healing was by no means unmitigated praise and thanksgiving. The parents are afraid, and in their blindness the Pharisees publicly denounce the healing because it happened on the Sabbath. They are put in their place, however, by the one who was healed: "Whether he is a sinner, I do not know; one thing I know, that though I was blind, now I see." This healing narrative expresses why healings are a sign of Jesus' relationship with God—"We know that God does not listen to sinners"—and the authorities cannot say anything further in rebuttal. All they can do is insult the healed man and cast him out.

11:1–46: Lazarus. In keeping with the view held at the time of Jesus, the difference between raising someone from the dead and a healing is only relative. Of particular significance here are the conversations. The slight rebuke by Martha ("if you had been here, my brother would not have died") is followed by a statement of trust: "Even now I know that whatever you ask from God, God will give you." And if she offers merely an evasive answer to Jesus' affirmation—"I know that he will rise again in the resurrection"—this dialogue seeks to express the following: This woman cannot believe that her brother, who is already lying in the tomb, will be made alive again; nevertheless, she has kept her trust in Jesus. The personal trust in Jesus remains unbroken, even in the face of death. This is the meaning of the saying in the middle of this conversation: "I am the resurrection and the life; he who believes in me, though he die, yet shall he live" (v. 25).

Summary. In the healings, Jesus works "the works of my Father." They are not merely "signs" pointing to the work of redemption as such; they are a major part of his ministry. They are based on what the Psalms express about sorrow and transforming suffering; they have their prehistory in the healing narratives of the Old Testament. They point up the difference between a *faith* performed by the head only and a *trust* embracing the whole person. In the healing narratives, the emphasis rests upon what transpires between the sick person and the one who reaches out in compassion. The miracle takes place only where the response to this compassion is unconditional trust. From this arises the new relationship between the one healed and the healer.

Other Acts of Jesus

Jesus' acts can be divided into three groups:

(1) 2:1–11 (the wedding at Cana) and 2:13b–17 (the temple cleansing) represent accounts from the early part of Jesus' life, before the actual beginning of his ministry.

(2) The two accounts in the middle, in 6:5–15 (the feeding of the five thousand) and 6:16–21 (the rescue from the storm), deal with salvation from kinds of situations other than sickness; thus they supplement the healings (following Ps 107).

(3) Toward the end of this first part, there are two acts, 12:1–11 (the anointing at Bethany) and 12:12–19 (the entry into Jerusalem); 13:1–19 (the footwashing) represents a parabolic action which is already part of the conclusion.

The footwashing, introducing the farewell discourses, needs to be addressed in particular here. As an act of service, a *diakonia,* it portrays Jesus' concluding exhortation to his disciples and hence points to a fundamental attitude that ought to determine their entire lifestyle. It is noteworthy that the exhortation is given in the form of an action. Accordingly, the church as a whole should become as one who serves. But when the church's chief office became that of the *episkopos,* the overseer, and the office of the *diakonos* was subordinated to it, the church chose a direction that did not follow the intent of this parabolic action of Jesus. The later structure of church government sharply contrasts with his action.

Two Accounts from the Early Part of Jesus' Ministry: 2:1–11 and 2:13–22

The oral tradition about Jesus, like the early historical narratives of the Old Testament, began with family narratives (Luke 1, 2). The turning of water into wine takes place in the context of a family celebration; Jesus himself attributes no special significance to this act (2:24).

The incident on the way to Jerusalem is also an early account: Jesus is gripped with anger over the profaning of the temple. His action is akin to the work of the prophets of judgment.

The Feeding of the Five Thousand and the Rescue from the Storm: 6:5–21

Chapter 6 mentions further difficulties from which Jesus saves, in which he helps. By means of these examples the evangelist intends to show that Jesus' comprehensive, helping, and preserving intervention is an essential part of his salvific work.

6:5–15: The feeding. As the one who provides for his own, he is sent by his Father for this hour. He represents the God who blesses. In this act he recalls the provision of manna for the people in the wilderness. Yet just as he was usually able to heal only *one* person in the case of the healings from sickness, so he is also able to feed the hungry only with *one* meal. Nevertheless, he can demonstrate thereby that miracles also occur in the present. Here, too, the decisive thing is trust: Your heavenly Father provides for you. This narrative is paralleled by John 21:1–14, Peter's catch of fish.

6:16–21: The rescue from the storm. This account, too, is a kind of parabolic action, and the predicament here is a human situation as well: "Some went down to the sea in ships" (Ps 107:23–32). It speaks of an endangering of the person in travels by land, by sea, and in the air, and here too Jesus calls for trust: "It is I; do not be afraid." When the disciples see Jesus walking on the water, when he draws near them and they reach the shore immediately, he shows them the presence of God, parabolically, in life-threatening dangers.

Since the two accounts of salvation from distress are framed by two healings before and two after, what is presented here is the work of God in the ministry of Jesus as the one who heals, blesses, and protects in every area of life.

The healings are typical miracle stories. They are not so because they narrate "supernatural" deeds; as elsewhere in the Bible, the concept of the "supernatural" is inappropriate and wrong here. "Supernatural" would be what transcends creation, what is outside creation, but this is not in keeping with biblical thought. The healing power of the creator is at work *precisely* in the miracles of healing; Jesus said, "My Father is working still, and I am working" (5:17).

From the perspective of the one who is sick, the experience of a wondrous healing is part of his life story. As the one who is healed, he is able to recount it later. This encompasses the earlier time of suffering, the low point in his illness (when the physicians had already given up on him), and the wonderful transformation into recovery. A miraculous healing is always special and rare. This special event, which is experienced as a miracle by the one who was healed and for which he gives thanks, is remembered as such. This parallels the psalms of lament and of thanksgiving. Psalm 77:12–20 shows what the Gospels mean by miracles.

Jesus' Speeches

The speeches of Jesus in the Gospel of John are not "speeches" in terms of rhetoric. Jesus' discourse is not a speech from up on a podium or a pulpit. When Jesus speaks, he is on the same level as his audience, regardless of whether they are adherents or opponents. On account of his mission, Jesus is always vulnerable in speaking. As the incarnate one, he is their equal who does not want to have an advantage over his hearers; he is always exposed to their questions and challenges. When they turn away from his discourse (6:60), he has to let them depart. His speaking is part of the humiliation of the Son of God.

Conversations with Individuals

Conversations with individuals are very significant in the Gospel of John. They are indispensable for Jesus' type of ministry. While no verbatim records have been handed down to us, the evangelist does indicate by means of several examples how important such conversations were. This is already demonstrated in the fact that Jesus' speaking in the Gospel begins with two conversations with individuals. The most important aspect here is that Jesus thereby places himself on a par with those he addresses. He knows that he himself does not have the power to bring about a change in those addressed by him. He could never have used the term "conversion," a result of the motif of "the Son's relationship with the Father" (cf. pp. 29–31). He desires only to do what his Father wants, and he does not decide that. Hence, Jesus never applies pressure in his conversations. He knows that God alone can bring about a transformation, though he is not obligated to do so.

The conversations also demonstrate that Jesus addressed the people in their sphere of life: Nicodemus as a scribe and the Samaritan woman as a simple country woman. In both conversations Jesus does not answer questions directly; the answers are merely alluded to, or they remain deliberately concealed. The conclusion of ch. 4 indicates that the Samaritan woman was nevertheless moved by what she heard; it points the way from the conversation with the individual to those with the inhabitants of the town. They become receptive to what the woman tells. Here the beginnings of tradition are shown.

In the final healing narrative (11:20–28), conversations with individuals become prominent once again. If Jesus asks too much of the two women in his demands for faith here, hidden in this is the recognition that such faith is meant to grow and that personal trust is the decisive thing in this growth, even if they cannot yet comprehend everything at this time. Martha and Mary express that this trust in Jesus remains unbroken, even if Lazarus's death were final. This conforms to Jesus' saying, "he who believes in me, though he die, yet shall he live" (11:25).

Jesus' conversation with his brothers (7:1–13) has affinities with the conversation with individuals. His brothers intend to prompt him toward a public ministry, and they call on him to appear in Judea at an approaching festival. Jesus rejects this because his time has not yet come. That is to say, he is focusing on a time different from the one his brothers have in mind. When he still goes to Jerusalem, although in private, it indicates that his time in public will be different from what his brothers desired. In the conversation with his brothers Jesus chose the nonviolent way that the prophets had modeled.

Dialogues Associated with an Action

The conversations held in the context of healings should be considered conversations with individuals, although they constitute only brief statements.

Other conversations in conjunction with an action are the following: The call of the disciples (1:35–51) contains some statements made by Jesus and by the disciples; they are part of the action and are not a self-contained conversation. This also applies to 2:1–11. John 2:18–22 is probably an addition belonging to the controversy dialogues. In other instances, too—for example in 12:1–8 and 13:1–8—exchanges of words are part of the action. This holds true for Peter's confession in 6:66–71 as well. In the Gospel of John, the conversation bears the same significance as in the Old Testament.

Independent Discourses:
The Farewell Discourses, Chapters 13–16 and 17

The real locus of the independent discourses of Jesus is the complex of the farewell discourses in chs. 13–16. They are clearly different from the conversations with individuals, even if they are interspersed with occasional words by one of the disciples. Before the farewell discourses, the conversational form is the decisive feature in the Gospel. There are also the two parables in 10:1–18 and 15:1–8. These are, however, essentially developments of a comparison.

The farewell discourses. Chapter 12 contains the statement "I have come to this hour" (v. 27). It is also the hour of his farewell from the disciples. The farewell discourses are preceded by the parabolic action of the footwashing, whose meaning is developed in the words of farewell. Through this demonstration of service, Jesus provides the disciples with the new commandment to love one another, as he has loved them (13:34–35). The basis for the commandment is the love that Jesus has shown his disciples.

Like the footwashing scene itself, so also the words following it belong to the context of the household, the family and its sphere of life: the Father's house, going away and coming back, as well as being united in the Father's house. Hence, the farewell discourses likewise are words spoken to the particular situation. As Tobit 4 shows particularly well, the blessing, linked with an admonition, has its place in the farewell (especially in the case of a son leaving his father's house). The admonition is contained in the parabolic action of the footwashing, alongside the love commandment. This ushers in the farewell discourses, which belong to the semantic field of blessing, rather than to that of mission, tasks, and duties. Now Jesus is leaving them, but they will be reunited in the Father's house (14:2, 3). This part concludes with the pronouncement of peace; it speaks of the peace in the sheltering house of the Father. Blessing and peace belong together.

15:1–17: The vine and the branches; abiding in God's love. The farewell discourses are shaped by the semantic field of blessing, peace, and abiding. John 15:1–8 develops the metaphor of the vine and the branches. In ch. 14 it is the peace of the sheltering house of the Father; by comparison, ch. 15 speaks of the disciples' work after Jesus' departure. They are to produce fruit, and their work is to be effective. But this is possible only in their abiding relationship with their Lord. When Jesus chooses the metaphor of the vine and the branches precisely here, in his farewell, there is a direct connection with the parables of growth in the other Gospels. Here the evangelist does not explicitly articulate the great commission, "Go into all the world," for the important thing for him is to express that what Jesus intended to bring to humans, the reason the Father sent him, cannot be propagated through human activity and human effort. It will grow. Therein lies a gentle critique of the understanding of community as found in the Acts of the Apostles, where everything depends upon human activity. (It is possible that 15:2–3 is an addition.)

15:18–16:33: Announcement of persecutions, warning, and consolation. Not until now, enveloped in this affirmation of blessing, does Jesus speak of the dangers to which the disciples will be exposed. But their sorrow is to turn into joy. The conclusion is given in the pronouncement of peace in 16:33: "In the world you have tribulation. . . ."

John 17. John 17:1–26 is a broadly developed reflection on the farewell prayer of Jesus. The actual prayer comprises only parts of vv. 1, 4, 5, 6, 12, 15, 24.

1: "Father, the hour has come; glorify thy Son."

4: "I glorified thee on earth."

5: "And now, Father, glorify thou me."

6: "I have manifested thy name to the men whom thou gavest me; . . . and they have kept thy word."

12: "I have guarded them, and none of them is lost."

15: "I . . . pray . . . that thou shouldst keep them from the evil one."

24: "Father, I desire that they also, whom thou hast given me, may be with me where I am."

That John 17 as a whole is not a prayer can be seen in the many repetitions and in many of the sayings that depart from the form of prayer, for instance, v. 3, a saying that explains the meaning of eternal life and in

which Jesus speaks of "Jesus" in the third person. It
further becomes apparent that in the prayer itself, con-
gruent with the farewell context, Jesus only petitions
God to guard from the evil one those who have been left
behind, so that they might be reunited with him. The
petition for them to be one, for unity, occurs only in
the expansion, however, and within that it occurs five
times, in 17:20, 21, 22, 23. Furthermore, the goal of
knowing God is found only in this expansion, namely,
in the words of the recognition formula, as in Ezekiel.

Thus it is to be assumed that the expansion was
preceded only by Jesus' brief petition to God in the hour
of farewell from the world (vv. 1, 4–6, 12, 15, 24). The
expansion was added in a later situation in which the
unity of the community was threatened and "knowledge of God" was particularly important.

The Gospel of John apart from
the Controversy Dialogues

Only if the Gospel is read apart from the controversy
dialogues does the impression of a continuous account
arise, which leads, from the outset, to the passion narrative. The account as a whole is an event whose goal
is the passion narrative.

In this way only does the structural function of the
travel references become clear. The Gospel delineates
the way in which Jesus acted and spoke. There are
events and conversations en route, and these references
give the situations in which they occurred. By means of
notes appended to the references, the situations are
often spelled out more specifically. The travel references are missing from the controversy dialogues and
from ch. 17. Thus, the Gospel proceeds as follows:

The prologue (1:1–18), prefacing the whole Gospel,
yet already implying its major sections, is followed by
the introduction, the account of John (1:19–28, 34) and
the call of the first disciples (1:35–51).

The two accounts of the wedding at Cana (2:1–11) and the driving of the traders from the temple belong to an early period of Jesus' ministry (his mother and brothers travel with him). Here, too, are the first of the travel references (2:12–14), which are characteristic of Jesus' journey from this point to the end, and the first of the accounts on the reaction to Jesus' ministry (2:23–25), which recur time and again on this journey.

There follow two conversations with individuals, Nicodemus (3:1–12) and the Samaritan woman (4:1–16) (cf. pp. 15f. on their significance); this, in turn, is followed by an account of the results (4:39–42).

Two healings follow, at intervals: of the official of Capernaum (4:46–54) and of the sick man at the pool of Bethesda (5:1–16). The relationship between the two and 6:5–20 becomes clear only when the long controversy dialogue intervening in 5:17–47 is bracketed.

Then follow two accounts of deliverance from other troubles, namely, the feeding (6:5–15) and the rescue from the storm (6:16–21). Travel references have been inserted before and after these references, in 6:1–4 and 6:21–24. Peter's confession (6:66–71), which concludes the section composed of chs. 1–6, is separated from the rest by the extensive controversy dialogue in 6:25–65.

The section composed of chs. 7–13 begins with the conversation with the brothers (7:1–13); Jesus decides against a public appearance. From this arises the third controversy dialogue in 7:14–29, followed by the account of results. Then comes 7:37–39 ("On the last day of the feast . . .") and the reactions by the people (7:40–44), then by the officers (7:45–49) and Nicodemus (7:50–52). Here is inserted the story about Jesus and the adulterous woman (8:1–11). It is followed, without context, by the controversy dialogue in 8:12–59. The story continues in 9:1ff. with a healing.

The section composed of chs. 9–11 is framed by the two further healings: that of the one born blind (9:1–38) and the resurrection of Lazarus (11:1–46). In between is the parable of the Good Shepherd (10:1–18). This is followed by the fifth controversy dialogue in 10:22–59. The text concludes with the Sanhedrin's resolution to put Jesus to death (11:47–53), which leads into the passion account.

Chapter 12 contains two contrasting expressions of homage: the anointing at Bethany (12:1–8) and the entry into Jerusalem (12:12–19).

In 13:1–11 the footwashing and two announcements (Judas and Peter) prepare the way for the passion narrative, which then begins with the farewell discourses and the farewell prayer. The briefer texts between the longer ones are mostly either travel references or reports of the effects of Jesus' words and actions.

If the Gospel without the controversy dialogues in chs. 5–8 and 10 and without the speech supplements makes such a different impression, the main reason is that without them the acts (events) and words of Jesus are roughly balanced. (The controversy dialogues also include 2:18–21, an announcement of Jesus' death and resurrection in the form of a controversy dialogue.)

More important, however, is that *without* the controversy dialogues, there are only scant traces of gnostic expansions and derivations in the Gospel. Only in speech supplements and in the prologue are there a few gnostic statements. Thus it is no longer possible to speak of the influence of gnostic thought and teaching on the *entire* Gospel. Such influence is limited to the particular complex of controversy dialogues and isolated verses inserted later. The Gospel without this complex provides the story of Jesus of Nazareth *without gnostic influence.*

Excursus:
Event and Interpretation in the Gospel of John

In contrast to the Synoptics, the Gospel of John is interspersed throughout with interpretations, as is, for instance, the book of Deuteronomy as compared with the books of Exodus and Numbers. Here event and interpretation often merge. (Commentaries do not appear alongside the historical books until early Judaism.) Speeches represent a particular form of interpretation, both in the historical books (Deuteronomy, Joshua) and in the Gospel of John. Thus Jesus' discourses interpret his parables and parabolic actions. One complex in the Gospel of John forms an exception to this: the controversy dialogues in chs. 5–10 (excluding 9). Although they contain events as well, these are only window dressing and a frame for the dialogues. The latter are not concerned with events, but rather with assertions and their challenges. This can already be observed from the fact that they are not found in the context of travel references; that is, they are not events on a journey. Rather, the issue is the contrast between two groups. This is where we encounter most of the sayings that are recognized as gnostic statements. Elsewhere these are touched on only occasionally.

3

The Controversy Dialogues

Introduction

The controversy dialogues in 5:17–47, 6:25–65, 7:14–30(36), 8:12–59, and 10:22–39 are a foreign element in the Gospel of John. They are conspicuous in their context, in depicting "Jesus" and "the Jews" as partners in these controversy dialogues, but these are code names. Those speaking in these names are representatives of two groups hostile to one another long after Jesus' death. They belong more to early church history than to the Gospel of John.

It is important to distinguish between an earlier and a later layer, however, because contrasts in the contents call for it. In the earlier layer, the language corresponds entirely with that used in the rest of the Gospel. In the later layer, it is possible to recognize gnostic influence in motifs that can be characterized as gnostic.

Since the motifs are mixed up with one another and the individual statements are largely lacking in context, it is not possible to provide a structured overview of the individual dialogues.

They must be called controversy dialogues because the contrast frequently escalates to the point of insult and condemnation. This cannot be found elsewhere in the Gospel. Moreover, they differ substantially from the other conversations in the Gospel, just as in the book of Job the speeches of Elihu differ from those of the other friends.

Preliminary Remarks on Methodology

If the five controversy dialogues are read in succession, this first impression arises: Larger contexts occur only rarely, though the motifs are often repeated. The meaning of a statement usually does not arise from the uncertain context in which it is found; rather, it is necessary to look for its context in the scattered statements associated with the same motif.

This is quite evident in the narrative framework, which is composed almost solely of identical statements, as well as in the Jews' intention to put Jesus to death. They form a pattern of consistently identical statements, like a *cantus firmus.*

This can also be seen in the dialogues themselves. They consist of relatively few motifs, which recur in sentences of identical or similar wording. They pose difficulties when, in the context of one motif (e.g., Father-Son), sentences of other motifs are inserted, so that the main motif remains undeveloped and instead is torn apart, as in 5:19–30. Sometimes the motifs are so interwoven that they cannot be separated at all or only with difficulty. The emphasis in the interpretation, then, must focus on the motifs. This is confirmed when a motif consists of only one statement—for instance, "and they will die in their sins" or "and I give them eternal life"—which is found at various points and hence can only have been inserted subsequently. For this reason, it is impossible to attribute each of the five segments entirely to the earlier or to the later layer; this is possible only for the motifs. In many cases, statements of the earlier layer were adopted by the later, albeit with modifications, or, conversely, statements of the later layer were inserted into the earlier. The process of layering can be observed from changes such as these. In this connection, the broader contexts in which the main motifs are developed help in distinguishing between them. The same contextual confusion can be found in the later Mandaean writings.

Broader Contexts

In 5:17–47	Broader contexts are found in the relationship of the Son to the Father (5:19–30) and in the witness/testimony (5:31–47).
In 6:25–65	The bread of life (6:25–36; 6:51a–58).
In 7:14–30	Accusation and defense (7:19–24).
In 8:12–59	Establishment of opposites (8:23–26, 33–46).
In 10:22–39	My works bear witness to me (10:25–30, 32–38).

Chapter 5 belongs almost entirely to the earlier layer, as do ch. 7 with the main motif and ch. 10. The later layer is represented by ch. 8, the establishment of opposites, and ch. 6, the bread of life, eternal life.

In the earlier layer, the main concern of the two motifs is that of legitimizing the work and words of Jesus; the later is concerned with establishing an exclusive contrast in two groups whose spokespersons are designated "Jesus" and "the Jews."

The Earlier Layer

In the presentation of the Son's relationship with the Father, the most important aspect is that the Father sent the Son, and the Son understands himself to be sent from the Father. This is a personal and historical relationship that corresponds to the language of the Old Testament: The one sent by God understands himself to be in line with the prophets, who also perceived themselves to be called by God. The same is true in both instances; like the prophets, Jesus is not concerned with his own affairs and his own glory but with God's affairs and God's glory. All of these statements could just as well be part of the Gospel.

The witness motif has close affinities to that of the Son's relationship with the Father. There are several testimonies; the most important is God's testimony for Jesus, the works in which the Father grants him success. They indicate, above all, that he does them in the name of God and that God affirms Jesus in them. In every presentation of this motif, the statements are shaped by language and thinking rooted in the Old Testament. The Father loves the Son; the Son trusts him in all things and listens to what he tells him.

Chapter 7 contains a controversy dialogue in terms of accusation and defense, in which the arguments are clear, concrete, and reasonable to everyone. It has no parallel in the other controversy dialogues. This is the only one that arises from a situation. It is possible that it was an independent unit at one time and that there were several of this type. Detached from the complex of the controversy dialogues as handed down, it could have been part of the story of Jesus of Nazareth.

In ch. 10 the significance of the works for Jesus' ministry is emphasized once again.

The Later Layer

The characteristic motif for the later layer is the establishment of contrasts. It addresses itself more to unbelief than to belief. The opponents are told, "You know neither me nor the Father." Most of the statements express opposites: "You are from below, I am from above; you are of this world, I am not of this world." As he originates from his Father, so they originate from their father, the devil. In this regard, the later layer betrays an unmistakably gnostic influence. It originates in dualistic thought, in which two separate realms determine reality: "from below—from above." If the words of Jesus invite to salvation ("If any one is thirsty, let him come to me"), "Jesus" in the later layer does exactly the opposite: he repels and excludes.

The motif of the establishment of contrasts is convincing evidence that what "Jesus" says in the statements associated with this motif were not the words of Jesus of Nazareth. On his journey he did not repel and exclude. The conversations with individuals demonstrate this, as do the I-am sayings.

Another main motif is the thematic complex bread of life, eternal life, and judgment. The stylistic form hyperbole is particularly prominent here. The simple events bound up with the soil and with life are exaggerated in all directions, to the point of unreality, of speculation, which is in stark contrast to the Old Testament. Manna is of little value; what is important is the bread of life that suffices into eternity. Those believing in Jesus do not die, nor do they face the judgment; they already share in eternal life. The human being is no longer a creature limited by birth and death; Abraham is eternal, as is Jesus, and the believers are immortal.

In the statements of the later layer, the language and thinking of the Old Testament are left behind. These exaggerations are not part of the journey that Jesus took in the brief periods of his ministry. They belong to the interpretation of the story of his ministry. We are not contesting that controversy dialogues had a place in Jesus' ministry. He encounters rejection and opposition during his mission, as the example of ch. 7 shows. In the later layer of the controversy dialogues, however, this is not the issue; rather, the issue is one of gaining an interpretation of Jesus' life and ministry, derived not from dates and facts of this journey but from an understanding of the world and of reality drawn from another origin and imposed upon the life and ministry of Jesus.

For this reason, these controversy dialogues of the later layer are not integrated into the structure of accounts and itineraries. Instead, they stand apart, having arisen from later reflection.

The Motifs of the Earlier Layer

The Son's Relationship with the Father

The Son's relationship with the Father is not merely one motif among others. The earlier layer is completely governed by it. It is developed in several submotifs, with frequent references to them in subordinate clauses.

The most important submotif is that Jesus is sent by God and perceives himself as sent from God, just as the prophets knew they were sent by God. Like the prophets, he received a mission from God.

The phrase "he who sent me" (or something similar) is found ten times (5:30, 36f.; 6:38, 57; 7:16, 18, 28f.; 8:16, 18, 42).

> 5:30; 6:38, 56f.—Jesus determines to do the will of him who sent him.
> 5:36—"the works . . . bear me witness that the Father has sent me."
> 7:16; 8:38—"My teaching is not mine" (cf. also 12:44–50).
> 7:18—He is seeking God's glory, not his own.
> 7:28f.—"he who sent me is true."
> 7:29—"I come from him, and he sent me" (cf. also 8:42).
> 8:29—"He who sent me is with me; he has not left me alone."
> Jesus trusts in him.

All of these passages speak of a historical event. That God sent Jesus was an event in time, just as he had sent the prophets at a specific point in time. And it was a personal event; the relationship between the Father and the Son is personal (though this is not the case in the later layer). The Father entrusts something to him and supports him in it; the Son trusts in him, just as in the farewell discourses. What Jesus says and does is based upon what the Father has told and shown him.

The descent of the Son of man from heaven is something different. It is a gnostic-mythical conception that does not denote a historical act; it is not based upon a personal relationship between the Father and the Son:

> 6:33—"that which comes down from heaven, and gives life to the world."
>
> 6:50, 51a, 58—"the bread which comes down from heaven."

It is also part of these developments that Jesus works in agreement with God: "My Father is working still, and I am working" (5:17). He does not do his own will and does not seek his own glory; he works in the name of his Father. The Father shows him everything and leads his followers to him; he causes his work to succeed. The Father is with him, does not leave him alone; this brings about the relationship of trust between Father and Son. This relationship has its parallel in the relationship of the one praying to God in the Psalms: from God, direction and protection; from the human, trust and obedience.

Neither the motif as a whole nor the submotifs indicate any trace of mythical, mystical, or specifically gnostic language. The roots of this language lie in the Old Testament.

If the statements developing the Son's relationship are read in context, it is difficult to ignore the fact that the mutuality of the work of the Father and the Son takes place in a temporal process. "The Father . . . shows him all that he himself is doing." It is also a temporal process in terms of the Son paying attention to what the Father does: "the Son can do nothing of his own accord, but only what he sees the Father doing" (5:19). This is also the reason it must be a multifaceted activity, a diversity of word and action arising on his journey among people. The task that the Father assigns to the

Son whom he sends means primarily only these words and actions of the Son during his earthly journey. There is no reference here at all to redemption through his suffering and death. If the purpose of Jesus' coming to earth, the purpose of his incarnation, is seen only, or almost only, in his suffering, death, and resurrection, such explanations do not agree with the Gospel. The Father sends Jesus to people in order to minister among them. That Jesus' actual work of redemption consists of his suffering, death, and resurrection is not expressed in the Father's task given to the Son. Conversely, the Son is not given the task of proclaiming a doctrine. A task such as this is not even implied. Rather, what emerges from the Son's relationship with the Father is that the Father tells him each time what he is to tell others, depending on the situation. This does not call for a coherent doctrine or teaching. The same was true of the prophets.

The Witness

Witnessing likewise is a temporal-historical event; it is dialogical. This is true of John's witness for Jesus, as well as of the Scriptures' witness for him, but it is also true when God vindicates him by granting success to his works. This is precisely what the Gospel expresses when effective healings convince his contemporaries that Jesus' ministry is linked with God (cf. p. 27f.). They testify "that the Father has sent me" (5:36; 8:18).

The Works

"The works that I do in my Father's name, they bear witness to me" (10:25). "I have shown you many good works from the Father" (10:32), to which Jesus adds that if they do not believe him they should at least believe his works and thereby recognize that he is working in the name of God (10:37, 38). It is particularly important to note here that, by referring to the works he has shown, Jesus can only have meant those done before witnesses in his earthly ministry, thus especially—but not only—the healings. There is no reference here to his redemptive work in his suffering and death. The pericope 10:22–39, especially vv. 33–38, is mainly concerned with the works.

The works motif is very closely linked with the motif of the Father-Son relationship. They are also closely linked in ch. 5; in both instances they belong to the earlier layer. They provide the answer to the question of the Jews whether Jesus is the Messiah (10:24). The response changes the question: The works authenticate Jesus, though not as the Messiah of Jewish conception but as the one who in his works is one with the Father.

The Glory

This, too, is a recurring motif and is closely connected to the Son's relationship with the Father.

> 5:41—"I do not receive glory from men."
> 5:44—"How can you believe, who receive glory from one another and do not seek the glory that comes from the only God?"
> 7:18—"He who speaks on his own authority seeks his own glory; but he who seeks the glory of him who sent him is true, and in him there is no falsehood."
> 8:49—"but I honor my Father."
> 8:50—"Yet I do not seek my own glory; there is One who seeks it and he will be the judge."
> 8:54—"If I glorify myself, my glory is nothing; it is my Father who glorifies me."

Accusation and Defense

Only 7:19–24 represents a legal controversy, in which Jesus levels an accusation against his opponents and defends his action. Jesus accuses his opponents of not observing the very law they hold in such high regard and objects that he is indeed justified to heal "a whole person" on the Sabbath if it is permissible to circumcise a person on the Sabbath. At the conclusion, he admonishes them to judge with right judgment. John 7:19–24 is a genuine controversy dialogue. In it the two parties are Jesus of Nazareth and his Jewish opponents. It arises from a situation—one of Jesus' healings on the Sabbath, for which he is being attacked. It may be part of the story of Jesus of Nazareth that preceded the later controversy dialogues in the present text. John 7:19–24 is framed by vv. 16–18 and 28–29, which belong to the Father-Son motif.

There are no motifs of the later layer in the controversy dialogue of 7:14–29.

Proclamation, Individual Sayings

Only in 8:12 does an I-am saying introduce a controversy dialogue.

> 8:12—"Again Jesus spoke to them, saying, 'I am the light of the world.'"

There are other I-am sayings, though they are not found only in controversy dialogues:

> 6:35, 41—"I am the bread of life."
> 7:37ff.—I am (the living water, cf. 4:10). "If any one thirst, let him come to me and drink."
> 10:11—"I am the good shepherd."
> 11:25f.—"I am the resurrection and the life."
> 14:6—"I am the way (and the truth, and the life)."
> 15:1, 5—"I am the vine."

Many interpreters assume that the I-am sayings originally formed an orally transmitted series. Individual I-am sayings are thought to have been removed from this series and put into a different context. The two parables in chs. 10 and 15 need to be excluded, in this case; in all likelihood, they originated together with their I-am sayings. It is further possible that some of the other I-am sayings were also parts of parables. This is plausible because these discourses not only develop their I-am sayings but interpret them at the same time. If there was a series of I-am sayings, it may also be assumed that there was an independent group of parables, analogous to the group of parables in the Synoptics.

What all of the I-am sayings have in common is that they intend to give or promise something. Common to all is that they compare Jesus with something that is alive, something belonging to creation, a necessity of life.

Since they are mostly individual sayings, they preserve the fact that in the early tradition, oral or even written, individual sayings were a significant part of the proclamation of Jesus. Therefore they can be attributed to the early Jesus tradition.

To the extent that they are found in the controversy dialogues, all of these inviting and promising sayings of Jesus are part of the earlier layer. They are in sharp contrast to the isolating, condemning, excluding sayings of the later layer, for instance, "you will die in your sins." This can be seen explicitly in the way the parable of the Good Shepherd is reshaped into a contrasting saying: "because you do not belong to my sheep" (10:26).

The Specific I-Am Sayings

The I-am sayings in the Gospel of John are not all of one kind. Each of them must be studied in its own place and context.

> 8:12—"I am the light of the world; he who
> follows me will not walk in darkness
> (but will have the light of life)."

This saying stands on its own as an independent saying of Jesus, introduced by 8:12a: "Again Jesus spoke to them, saying." In response to the saying, the Pharisees attack him: "You are bearing witness to yourself" (8:13).

Here the author of the controversy dialogues seems to have had at hand an independent saying of Jesus from the tradition. It contains an invitation, together with a promise, whose reference point remains in the life of the here and now: Light will be shed on the path of the one who follows me; he will know where he is going and find his path. Hence, it belongs to the sayings of Jesus containing an invitation ("Come to me") and focuses on a this-worldly event, just as if someone in a dark cellar heard the words, "Wait, I am switching on the light for you!" Understood in this manner, this can be a saying spoken by Jesus.

10:11, 14—"I am the good shepherd."

John 10:1–18 represents one of the few independent discourses. It explains the comparison to the shepherd, which describes Jesus' relationship with his disciples or his adherents. He is not the owner, the master of the sheep; they are merely entrusted to him. He is only the shepherd; someone else is the master (cf. the motif of the Father-Son relationship). The comparison to the shepherd has affinities with the parable of the foot-washing. Jesus only wants to be the servant, the one leading the sheep, the one providing them with nourishment. But his serving goes to the utmost; if his function as shepherd should call for it, he will give his life for his sheep. This comparison refers to the incarnation and so is entirely in keeping with the direction of the Gospel.

10:9—"I am the door."

The comparison to the door is merely derived from its preceding context, not an independent comparison. It is explained in 10:1–2a: The shepherd enters the sheepfold by the door. He acts in keeping with the instructions given by the master and owner of the sheep; he is commissioned by God. Once again this is the motif of Jesus and the Father. Or is it a delimiting addition: "*only* by the door!*"?

15:1, 5—"I am the vine."

This is a simple though substantially expanded comparison, a promise, linked with an admonition that Jesus speaks in the farewell to his disciples. The analogy concerns God's beneficent action. The shepherd-flock comparison (ch. 10) concerned Jesus' journey with his disciples; now in the farewell, after Jesus' departure, the vine analogy concerns abiding together and bearing fruit. The converse could not be true.

The two comparisons in chs. 10 and 15 are so firmly integrated into the whole and so meaningfully correspond with one another that it can be said with certainty that both belong to the Gospel and originated in the sayings of Jesus of Nazareth.

11:25—"I am the resurrection and the life; he who believes in me, though he die, yet shall he live."

This saying is found in the account of the resurrection of Lazarus, in a conversation between Jesus and Martha. It can be explained adequately only by interpreting the chapter as a whole. In brief: Jesus provides Martha, who is questioning and doubting, the concealing or hidden answer that is typical for such conversations. It is not intended to be a logical answer but is meant to reinforce the confidence of the sister of the sick person. If the saying is understood in this manner, it is an integral, essential part of the account and thus of the action it reports, together with the explanatory statement: "he who believes in me, though he die, yet shall he live." This statement is juxtaposed with the saying in the gnostic expansion of v. 26, the promise of immortality. This contrast leads to the conclusion that Jesus' response in 11:25 is an essential part of the account of ch. 11 and hence of the Gospel.

6:35—"I am the bread of life; he who comes
to me shall not hunger, and . . . thirst."

This is as much a statement of invitation as others in the independent sayings. It contains a promise for life here and now. It addresses physical hunger and physical thirst. "Have you ever suffered hardship?" This interpretation is certain because the discourse follows the multiplication of the loaves.

The discourse in 6:31–58 is part of the controversy dialogues. Its composition is confused and awkward, made up of many pieces that match only in part, with many repetitions ("come down from heaven" seven times). In this discourse the "bread of life" saying occurs also in vv. 32, 33, 48–51 (four times), and 58 (twice); in addition, vv. 51–56 have "the bread . . . is my flesh."

This accumulation is conspicuous. It is a sort of treatise on the bread of life in which "the flesh" (Jesus) is added to the bread. The original independent saying has been changed into a tract.

In this entire discourse, the "bread of life" or the "true bread from heaven" is the means to obtain immortality, the *pharmakon athanasias*: vv. 32b, 40, 47, 50, 51, 58. Thus in v. 50, "that a man may eat of it and not die," and v. 51a, "if any one eats of this bread, he will live for ever." What is developed here is the gnostic-dualistic teaching of immortality.

This promise of eternal life is linked with a rejection that is plainly expressed twice. In v. 31 the Jews point to the manna in the wilderness. This is deliberately devalued. It was not "the true bread of life" (vv. 32–58), for those who ate it died. The true bread is the food from heaven (reiterated seven times), which is identified with Jesus: "he who eats my flesh" (vv. 51a, 57, 58). Like the manna in the wilderness, the bread Jesus distributed to the hungry is also devalued: "Do not labor for the food which perishes" (v. 27).

Both statements are in stark contrast to the Old Testament; they represent a devaluation of creation and of the creator. Detachment from history is merely the other side of rejecting the creator.

14:6—"I am the way (and the truth, and the life; no one comes to the Father, but by me)."

This metaphor is part of a conversation between Jesus and his disciples, in the context of his farewell. He is going back to his Father's house and will then take the disciples to that place (14:2). "And you know the way where I am going" (v. 4). Then (v. 6) Thomas interrupts him, "we do not know where you are going; how can we know the way?" and Jesus responds: "I am the way (, and the truth, and the life; no one comes to the Father, but by me)." "If you had known me, you would have known my Father also; henceforth you know him and have seen him" (v. 7).

Jesus' response consists of *one* sentence: "I am the way." It is the typically concealing response that is supposed to evoke reflection. An aid to reflection is given in the addition: "If you had known me, you would have known my Father." The intervening words were added later. The addition of "and the truth, and the life" serves no purpose here; it merely tops it off, as does the rejection, frequently encountered, that follows it: "no one . . . but . . ." The only thing that surprises and invites reflection is the response to the question by Thomas: "I am the way."

In this way—and only in this way, without the subsequent addition—is this saying firmly anchored both in the Gospel as a whole and in the context of the farewell. The addition only impedes the understanding of the saying.

The I-am sayings represent a group of sayings in which it becomes particularly apparent that they cannot be understood synchronically (as H. Thien argues) but only in the context of a *history* of tradition.

This is supported, for one thing, by the following: If they had originated synchronically, it would have to be assumed that the complete series of I-am sayings was composed at the same time (as in the case of the Beatitudes). They are, however, found in completely diverse contexts or as independent sayings without any context. This points to a nonsynchronic origin in a multifaceted history of tradition. This seems to me to be quite certain.

A further point can be adduced: It can also be observed in the brief, independent sayings of the Synoptics that they change in the history of their tradition; this is a very natural process. Either they are integrated into a larger unit (thus allowing their meaning to be changed) or they are expanded in many different ways, as is to be expected with brief sayings such as these. This is obviously what happened with some of the I-am sayings:

8:12—"I am the light of the world; he who follows me will not walk in darkness (but will have the light of life)." Only the phrase with "he who follows me" is necessary.

14:6—"I am the way (and the truth, and the life)."

7:37ff.—I am the living water (following 4:10). "If any one thirst, let him come to me and drink."

11:25f.—"I am the resurrection and the life; he who believes in me, though he die, yet shall he live (and whoever lives and believes in me shall never die)."

6:35—"I am the bread of life; he who comes to me shall not hunger . . . and thirst."

The two remaining sayings are part of a parable:

10:11, 14—"I am the good shepherd." Added later: "I am the door."

15:1, 5—"I am the vine, you are the branches."

Both forms may have existed alongside one another.

The I-am sayings are *not* self-revelatory, for Jesus is speaking in a concealing manner in them. What Jesus says here is precisely not, "I am the Messiah"; instead, he expresses what he is for those who listen to him and what he does or can mean to them, or simply what he can give them, what they have in him. Yet he does not say this plainly but only intimates it; those whom he addresses are to find it on their own. This is true of the I-am sayings as well as of the conversations. He wants to make his hearers take notice and reflect. Each of these statements is part of his offer and, as such, an invitation to entrust themselves to him. The offer consists of what every person needs in life: light, bread, life, direction, protection, growth, and yielding fruit. And if Jesus says in a concealed and enigmatic way, "I am all of this, you can have all of this in me," he simply means, "If you entrust yourselves to me, if you follow me, I am the one through whom you receive all of this."

This offer of Jesus in the I-am sayings contrasts with the demand for separation from others and the condemnation of others, as well as with promises of immortality that thereby forsake the ground of reality.

Announcement

Jesus' announcement of his death, in itself, is part of the Gospel (cf. Mark 14:41). Jesus announces his departure several times, as in 7:33f.: "I shall be with you a little longer, and then I go to him who sent me" (cf. 12:35f.). The assumption of two layers is confirmed by the fact that the same announcement is repeated in 8:21, though here with an addition: "and you will . . . die in your sin" (repeated in 8:24). The announcement itself belongs to the earlier layer, while the addition is part of the later one; it also occurs as an independent announcement to unbelievers.

The statement "My hour has not yet come" (2:4; 7:30; 8:20; 12:23–27; 13:1; 17:1) is an indirect announcement, together with the declaration that it is now here (12:23–27). This statement links the first part of the

Gospel with the passion narrative, and thus presupposes the joining of the two parts. From the beginning, Jesus focused on this hour. In contrast to the Synoptic Gospels, a conception appears that directs the Gospel of John as a whole. This statement is not gnostic, however.

Neutral Concepts

Some concepts that are not associated with a specific motif but occur in quite different contexts can only sometimes be attributed clearly to the earlier or later layer. For this reason I designate them as *neutral* concepts here.

Faith, Believing

The term is used very generally and imprecisely: to believe in someone, or just to believe. What predominates here is a primarily intellectual understanding: The people who witness a healing by Jesus form an opinion; that is, they either do or do not believe in him.

Conversely, there is an entirely different conception of "believing" in the healing narratives when one of those healed by Jesus believes in the one who healed him and a relationship of trust is thereby established.

One of the differences between the earlier and the later layer can be seen in the domination of the negative use in the later layer.

> 6:36—"But I said to you that you have seen me and yet do not believe" (cf. 8:24, 37).
> 10:25—"I told you, and you do not believe."
> 10:26—"but you do not believe, because you do not belong to my sheep."

Not believing is discussed in order to establish a contrast. Compare 8:24: "for you will die in your sins unless you believe that I am he" (cf. also 3:18).

Truth and Lie

Truth and lie are discussed mostly in the abstract, and hence mostly in the later layer. In 8:44–47 truth and lie are juxtaposed in order to establish a contrast in the sharpest of expressions.

In 14:6, "I am the way, and the truth, and the life" arises from the context of Jesus' original answer, "I am the way," analogous to the other I-am sayings. The two additions, "and the truth, and the life," yield no *meaning* in the context; here "truth" and "life" are positive principles used abstractly.

The Motifs of the Later Layer

Establishing a Contrast: Dualism

For the later layer, establishing a contrast is the most characteristic motif. If the statements of this motif are read on their own, one might be shocked by the intense separatism, like that seen among sects.

The audience's unbelief is recognized as a fact, as in 10:25: "I told you, and you do not believe."

A very long section of ch. 8 develops this motif: 8:23, 24, 34–47. The basic tone remains that of stating a case.

> 8:23f.—"You are from below, I am from above; you are of this world, I am not of this world" (cf. 3:12, 13, 20, 21, 31f., 36).
> 8:55—"But you have not known him; I know him."

This is a classic formulation of gnostic dualism, in which reality consists of two opposite realms and every person belongs either to the one or to the other. Statements with the I/you structure occur frequently in this motif.

8:23–24—This dualism substantiates what "Jesus" says to the "Jews": "where I am going, you cannot come," that is, into the realm of the divine, the eternal. Those addressed belong to another realm: "I told you that you would die in your sins." Their destiny in darkness is sealed because they do not believe in Jesus; nothing can be done to change this (6:36; 10:25f.). In contrast to this, Jesus says, If I now go to the Father, I will take you to myself.

8:34–47—To the Jews, who are proud to be free as sons of Abraham, he says: As sinners you are slaves, and only I can set you free. By intending to kill me you prove that you are not doing the works of Abraham. You really have another father whose works you do, the devil. This again is dualism in its starkest form: One's father is either God or the devil. The latter is a murderer from the beginning and the liar who has no share in the truth (8:44–47). You are not from God, he tells them; hence you are not able to understand me either.

A more blunt delineation of gnostic teaching cannot be imagined. It is in starkest contrast with what the Gospel of John says about Jesus. There is no common ground here. This is camouflaged in the text of ch. 8 because the dualistic statements, establishing a contrast, are frequently interspersed with statements belonging to the earlier layer. Or a statement of the earlier layer, such as "I speak of what I have seen with my Father," is supplemented with "and you do what you have heard from your father" (8:38). Yet even the recurring I/you sentence structure is characteristically concerned with establishing a contrast. There is no attempt at persuasion here at all. The contrast is fixed. In this case, there is no history either for believers or for unbelievers. The contrasting situation is already present and remains forever. Jesus' inviting proclamation in the individual sayings has no room here.

How differently the Gospel speaks of Jesus can be seen from the conversation with Nicodemus. It does not conclude with Nicodemus being persuaded by Jesus and by what he says. Yet Jesus does not reckon him among the unbelievers, nor does he tell him that he will die in his sins. He waits, and the remark in 7:50–52 indicates that Nicodemus is not found on the side of Jesus' opponents.

The Origin of Abraham (8:37–45)

The establishment of a contrast is also developed in the differing origins of the two parties: Jesus comes from the Father, to whom he will also return again. The Father has sent Jesus, accompanies his ministry, and makes sure that it is successful. In contrast, the Jews insist on their descent from Abraham. "Jesus" contests this: If Abraham were your father, you would have to love me. If you are bent on killing me, you are not Abraham's sons. Neither are you free as Abraham's sons; rather, you are slaves of sin, and only I can make you free. The physical descent from Abraham is disparaged and held to be of little value. The thinking behind this is ahistorical. Abraham's significance in the Old Testament and inclusion among his descendants are simply dismissed. The origin of the two parties in the controversy dialogue is something different for each. When the Jews say, "Abraham is our father," but also "We have one Father, even God," they have in mind (historical) descent from the progenitor and being God's creation respectively. "Jesus," however, has in mind "spiritual descent." They do not come from God because they do not love him. They are not Abraham's descendants because they are not doing his works. On the one hand, what is meant is creaturely-historical descent; on the other hand, it is spiritual descent, descent in terms of mind-set. The former is an Old Testament construct, the latter is gnostic. Add to this the excessive intensification: Your father is not Abraham but the devil, because you are doing the works of the devil. Thus "Jesus" also denies that the Jews are God's creation (8:47: "you are not of God"). The meaninglessness of creation and of creatureliness again is gnostic.

If this later layer contains the sharpest anti-Jewish statements in the Gospel of John, it is clear that both "the Jews" and "Jesus" are code names here. It is the conflict of two later orientations or groups. These abusive sayings about "the Jews" can in no wise have been spoken by Jesus.

Bread of Life, Eternal Life (John 6; cf. above p. 13f.)

Another contrast in Gnosticism is that of spirit and matter: "It is the spirit that gives life, the flesh is of no avail" (6:63). This contrast is developed in detail in ch. 6, together with many repetitions, and with some disruptions.

6:26ff.—Jesus answers the Jews who are seeking him, You are seeking me because you ate the bread and had your fill, not because you have seen a sign. He exhorts them in v. 27: "Do not labor for the food which perishes, but for the food which endures to eternal life." The one giving it to you is the Son of man. The Jews point to the miracle of the manna in the wilderness, in which they have seen the work of God. "Jesus" qualifies this: It is not Moses who gave you the bread but the Father *now* gives you the true bread from heaven. "I am the bread of life" who has come down from heaven and gives life to the world. He further qualifies the miracle of the manna: Your fathers ate the manna and died; I am the bread that has come down from heaven so that one may eat of it and *not* die. He who eats of this bread will live eternally. This is followed by several repetitions, including the devaluation of the miracle of the manna in vv. 49, 58. The excessive intensification typical of the later layer occurs again in v. 58: "he who eats this bread will live for ever, will not see death" (cf. 8:51; also 10:28; 6:40)—quite apart from the misunderstanding of the narrative of the rescue from death by starvation in the book of Exodus.

After the Jews note (8:52ff.) that Abraham and the prophets had died, there follows another intensification in v. 56: "Abraham rejoiced that he was to see my day." For one thing, this representation ignores the fact that the miracle of the manna meant salvation from death by starvation, and against the Old Testament it takes a low view of the bread that satisfies the hunger. Furthermore, the bread of life is intensified excessively, to the extent that it grants eternal life, and all who eat it will not experience death. Thus the human being ceases to be God's creature, for birth and death are part of creatureliness. Bread becomes "spiritual food," a medicine of immortality, a *pharmakon athanasias*. Furthermore, this intensification is not very effective as an argument: It is not possible to deny to "the Jews" that Abraham and the prophets died.

How important the affirmation of eternal life is in the later layer of the controversy dialogues can be seen in the frequent repetition of this statement:

3:15f.; 6:47f.—"he who believes has eternal life" (6:40; 3:36).
6:51—"if any one eats of this bread, he will live for ever" (6:54).
8:51—"If any one keeps my word, he will never see death" (10:28f.).

These statements do not refer to the resurrection from the dead but to immortality. That human existence encompasses death as much as birth is being denied here. After all, death has taken even those to whom the promise is made here that they will not die. It is also important to note that affirmations for *this* life do not occur. This-worldly life is irrelevant; nothing substantial happens in it.

The Flesh

An expansion within the motif of "the bread" is 6:51b–56: the flesh.

> 6:51b—" 'and the bread which I shall give for the life of the world is my flesh.' The Jews then disputed among themselves, saying, 'How can this man give us his flesh to eat?' "
>
> 6:53–56—"unless you eat the flesh of the Son of man and drink his blood, you have no life in you; he who eats my flesh and drinks my blood has eternal life. . . . For my flesh is food indeed, and my blood is drink indeed. He who eats my flesh and drinks my blood abides in me and I in him."

The entire expansion is merely an intensification of what has been said concerning the bread, as shown by the clumsy transition, "the bread . . . is my flesh." For this intensification, the words of distribution at the Lord's Supper are utilized. Doing so, however, removes the material, the "true flesh," and abstracts it from the event of the distribution at Jesus' farewell, a grave distortion of the text. It is being spiritualized to become a "medicine of immortality."

The reaction to this in vv. 59, 60 is understandable: "This is a hard saying." Here, too, it is impossible to attribute this gnostic thought to Jesus himself.

The Judgment

5:27—"[The Father] has given [the Son] authority to execute judgment." Hence his judgment is just.

5:30—"as I hear, I judge; and my judgment is just."

8:15f.—Jesus says, "You judge according to the flesh, I judge [i.e., condemn] no one." But then he continues, "Yet even if I do judge, my judgment is true, for it is not I alone that judge, but I and the Father who sent me." In the statement "I judge no one," the verb *krinein* has the sense of "condemn," as shown in 8:1–11.

In all these statements, including 5:30, "judging" denotes an occurrence in Jesus' life. Conversely, 5:24, "he who hears my word and believes . . . does not come into judgment," clearly refers to an event in the end times. This also applies to the two additions: in 5:25, "the hour is coming, and now is, when the dead will hear the voice of the Son," and in vv. 28, 29, "the hour is coming when all who are in the tombs will hear his voice and come forth . . . to the resurrection of life . . . [and] of judgment." In both statements it is the Son of man who conducts this judgment.

The last judgment is also meant in another group of additions, as in 6:39: "but raise it up at the last day" (also vv. 40, 44, 54). The conventional doctrine of the last things appears in both groups of additions: resurrection and judgment are events of the last days. This event character is forsaken completely in the supplement to the discourse in 3:19: "This is the judgment, that the light has come into the world, and men loved darkness rather than light." Yet another meaning of judgment is shown in Jesus' farewell in 12:31: "*Now* is the judgment of this world; now shall the ruler of this world be cast out" (italics added).

When the controversy dialogues arose, the meaning was still quite fluid; according to one view, there was a judgment by Jesus that occurred during his ministry, while, according to another, the judgment was carried out in Jesus' death and resurrection. Following 12:31 and 8:15f. the judgment completely loses its character as an event; in other words, it takes place in Christ's coming to earth. In both groups of additions, the conventional teaching of the last things is represented as in the Apostles' Creed. Furthermore, in gnostic thought the time of the judgment is irrelevant; judgment is a spiritual, timeless event.

Announcements

Several times Jesus predicts his death by means of the Johannine verb "to lift up," denoting both the exaltation on the cross and the "exaltation" to heaven. The announcement of his death, as such, is part of the tradition. "Do you take offense at this? Then what if you were to see the Son of man ascending where he was before?" (6:61f.; 12:32; cf. 3:14; 8:28: "When you have lifted up the Son of man, then you will know"). In addition, he predicts (as in the Synoptic Gospels) that one of his disciples will betray him (6:64).

Several times Jesus announces his departure, as in 2:18–20; 7:33f.: "I shall be with you a little longer, and then I go to him who sent me; you will seek me and you will not find me; where I am you cannot come" (cf. 12:35f.). It is characteristic and supports the assumption of two layers that the same announcement is repeated in 8:21, though here with an addition: "and [you will] die in your sin," which is then repeated yet again in 8:24. The announcement per se may belong to the earlier layer, the addition only to the later one. The addition also is presented as an independent announcement to unbelievers.

The announcements as such are not part of the controversy dialogues, though they occur between them and in association with them. It should also be remembered here that in gnostic thought there can be no such thing as announcements in the strictly historical sense, for time is not important; in this way one is to understand the frequently occurring phrase "the hour is coming, and now is." Time becomes relative; hence, there is also no more history.

The Questions of the Jews

1. The question of who Jesus is.
   2:18—"What sign have you to show us?" (cf. 6:30).
   8:19—"Where is your Father?"
   8:25—"Who are you?"
   10:24—"If you are the Christ, tell us plainly."

2. Other inquiries:
   6:28—"What must we do?"
   6:42—"How does he now say . . . ?"
   7:15—"How is it that this man has learning?" (cf. also 6:25, 42; 7:35; 8:22).

3. Replies and reproaches:
> 8:13—"You are bearing witness to yourself."
> 8:39—"Abraham is our father."
> 8:53—"Who do you claim to be?" (cf. also 6:52;
> 8:33, 41, 52, 53: "Are you greater than our father
> Abraham?")
> 10:33—"because you, being a man, make yourself
> God" (cf. 5:18).

4. Insults:
> 7:20—"You have a demon!"
> 8:48—"Are we not right in saying that you are a
> Samaritan and have a demon?"

What is conspicuous is that "the Jews" do not have a position and hence do not juxtapose the "I" of "Jesus" with a "we." They do not present the central Old Testament declarations about God (except by allusion in 10:33). They merely contradict "Jesus." A considerable number of questions are neutral, not polemical. In part, these are questions of interest in his person. There is a noticeable intensification, however; the questions become sharper in ch. 8, in keeping with that chapter's character.

On the whole, one gets the impression that the questions and objections are invented, completely different form the words and deeds of the Jews in the Gospel apart from the controversy dialogues, for the latter arise from the situation, which also provides them with their meaning. Indeed, the questions and objections in the controversy dialogues follow only one particular pattern. The true opponents are not at all the Jews who oppose Jesus in the rest of the Gospel.

The true interlocutors are two Christian groups quite some time after Jesus' death. For one of the groups, Jesus' relationship with God, as developed in the Father-Son motif, is characteristic. For the other group, this relationship should be aligned with gnostic-dualistic thought. One orientation corresponds with the knowledge of God in the Old Testament, while the other stands in opposition to it.

Additions to Discourses in the Gospel

3:11–21

earthly-heavenly	12: "If I have told you earthly things and you do not believe . . ." 13: Only he who descended from heaven can speak of heavenly things.
lifting up	14: Like the serpent in the wilderness, "so must the Son of man be lifted up."
eternal life	15: "that whoever believes in him may have eternal life." 16: "For God so loved the world that he gave his only Son."
independent saying	17: "not to condemn the world, but that the world might be saved through him."
judgment	18: "He who believes in him is not condemned; he who does not believe is condemned already." 19: "This is the judgment, that the light has come into the world, and men loved darkness rather than light."
light-darkness contrast	20: "Everyone who does evil hates the light." 21: "But he who does what is true comes to the light."

3:31–36

from above (cf. prologue)	31: "He who comes from above is above all; he who is of the earth . . . [speaks] of the earth." 32: "[He who comes from heaven] bears witness to what he has seen . . . , yet no one receives his testimony." 33: "he who receives his testimony sets his seal to this, that God is true." 34: "He whom God has sent utters the words of God."
Father-Son contrast	35: "the Father loves the Son, and has given all things into his hand." 36: "He who believes in the Son has eternal life; he who does not . . . the wrath of God rests upon him."

4:31–38

Father and Son	31–34: " 'Rabbi, eat.' . . . "I have food to eat of which you do not know. . . . My food is to do the will of him who sent me, and to accomplish his work." 35–37: " 'There are yet four months, then comes the harvest?' I tell you, . . . the fields are already white for harvest. . . . so that sower and reaper may rejoice together. . . . " 'One sows and another reaps.' " 38: "I sent you to reap that for which you did not labor."

12:20–50

the hour	23–30: "The hour has come. . . . He who loves his life . . . If any one serves me . . ."
	27: "Now is my soul troubled."
judgment	31–36: "Now is the judgment of this world, now shall the ruler of this world be cast out."

Three additions to discourses can clearly be recognized as such. They can be discerned, first, by the general lack of relationship among the individual statements and, second, by their almost always occurring in doublets, which have little or no variation between them. This applies to 3:11–21, 3:31–36, and 4:31–38. One gets the impression that they originated only because there was still room at the bottom of the papyrus folio or in the margin to fill with such additions. From the key words in the left hand column, it can be seen that almost all of them correspond to the motifs of the controversy dialogues and, apart from the Father-Son motif, to those of the later layer. A question remains only regarding 4:35 and 37, which is fragmented, and v. 38—the only statement referring to a sending out of the disciples and to a task given to them.

The pericope of 12:20–50 is a variant of Jesus' farewell. It also needs to be brought up here because 12:23–30 refers to the hour, which is frequently mentioned in the controversy dialogues: "My hour has not yet come." Now, in 12:23–30, it has come. And in 12:31–36, the language parallels that of the later layer: the judgment of the world occurs in Jesus' death (being lifted up); this is the last judgment, in which "the ruler of this world" comes to an end. The death of Jesus and the last judgment are simultaneous.

*Additions in 3:11–21, 3:31–36, and 4:31–38 and in
Parts of Chapter 12*

3:11–21	follows, as an addition, the conversation with Nicodemus, though it has nothing to do with the latter; it is composed of independent sayings.
3:31–36	follows the narrative about John without a link to it.
4:31–38	follows the narrative about the Samaritan woman, again without any link.
12:20–50	follows 12:12–19, the entry into Jerusalem, without any link; the pericope is composed of various independent segments.

These groups of texts are all found outside the controversy dialogues. Yet even in internally coherent additions, it is possible in some cases to distinguish between motifs of the earlier and the later layer. There are no additions to discourses in chapters containing controversy dialogues.

The "Father-Son" Motif

3:35—"the Father loves the Son, and has given all things into his hand" (=34).

4:32–34—"I have food to eat of which you do not know. . . . My food is to do the will of him who sent me."

In addition, there is another group of texts that occurs only twice (3:16f.; 12:44ff.): *God's love for the world.*

3:16—"For God so loved the world that he gave his only Son, that whoever believes in him should not perish but have eternal life."

3:17—"For God sent the Son into the world, not to condemn the world, but that the world might be saved through him" (Whether vv. 18–21 are part of it is questionable.)

12:44—"He who believes in me, believes not in me but in him who sent me."

12:45—"He who sees me sees him who sent me."

12:46—"I have come as light into the world, that whoever believes in me may not remain in darkness."

12:47—"If any one hears my sayings and does not keep them, I do not judge him; for I did not come to judge the world but to save the world."

This conspicuous group of sayings probably is an addition directed against the statements of the later layer and its denial of the world.

Summary: Comparing the Motifs of the Earlier and Later Layers

The examination has established an extensive contrast between the earlier and the later layers of the controversy dialogues. All of the motifs of the earlier layer may have been part of the story of Jesus of Nazareth. In any case, none of them is contradictory to it, which is not the case with the motifs of the later layer.

A comparison of the motifs of the earlier layer with those of the later layer indicates, first of all, that the initial motif of the earlier layer determines all the others: *the personal-historical relationship of the Father to the Son*, of the Son to the Father. Faith in Christ sees him as one who prays to his Father, to whom the Father shows everything, and whose trust is in the Father—and none of this is ever based on either a metaphysical relationship or one that is merely a poetical reflection. The interest of this earlier layer is focused solely upon the history in which God sent Jesus, in the same way that he had sent the prophets earlier, a history in which Jesus carried out the works of God. In the believing community this history continues through the Son, whose suffering (Isa 53) was for all and established the new people of God; they, like the incarnate Son of God, renounced power, just as the earlier prophets had done.

The statements in which "Jesus" speaks in the later layer contain *one* decisive motif as well. It does not refer to Jesus' relationship with God but strictly to the relationship of this "Jesus" to the partner in dialogue. It is an absolutely contrasting relationship, in which Jesus is not the one who invites, nor the one who is concerned with being understood. This contrast had always been and will always be. The intent of the discourse is dismissive, condemning, rejecting: "You are from below, I am from above."

The establishment of this contrast arises from a particular doctrine, namely, the spiritualizing of faith. Faith is no longer focused on history as an event but on being, *spiritual being*. This alone is true existence, this alone is "truth," this alone is essential: "It is the spirit that gives life, the flesh is of no avail" (6:63). It is a dualistic spiritualism; the human being belongs completely either to the one or to the other; he is either heavenly or earthly. He is from above or from below—creation is nonexistent. There is also no history (cf. the Abraham motif); there is only eternal being or nonbeing. The believer is promised immortality. The manna in the wilderness was worthless because it did not lead to immortality. Jesus' words and deeds on earth had no salvific significance. The only thing that has significance is his exaltation. Worthless, too, is Jesus' feeding of the hungry, for the bread he gives to them does not make them immortal.

Motifs of the Earlier Layer

Larger Contexts

5:17–30 The Father-Son relationship
5:31–47 The witness to the Son
7:19–24 Accusation and defense
10:25–30, 32–38 My works testify on my behalf

1. Father and Son: "I and the Father are one" (cf. pp. 29–31)
   My Father is working still and I am working.
   The Father has sent me (7:18–20).
   The Son cannot do anything of his own.
   The Father loves the Son; he shows him all things and
       has given all things into his hand (3:35).
   The Father judges no one, and neither do I.
   As the Father has life in himself, he has given life to the
       Son.
   I am not seeking my glory but the Father's
       (7:16–18; 8:49–55).
   Jesus draws his own to himself (his desire expressed
       to the Father).
   Further references: 3:35; 6:37–40, 41–46; 8:25f.,
       45–55; 10:25–30.

2. The witness to the Son (cf. p. 31)
   God bears witness to me (5:31f., 37, 38).
   The witness of John (5:33–35; also 8:13–19).
   My works bear witness to me (5:36; also 10:25–30,
       32–38).
   The Scriptures bear witness to me (5:30–40; also
       5:45–47: Moses is your accuser).

3. Accusation and defense (7:19–24)

4. Announcement
   "The hour has come" (12:23).
   "I shall be with you a little longer" (7:33f.; 12:35f.).

Motifs of the Later Layer

Larger contexts

8:23–36, 37–46: Establishing a contrast
6:25–36: The bread of life (also 51–58)

1. Establishment of contrasts (dualism)
   3:12f.—If I have told you of earthly/heavenly things . . .
       but he who descended from heaven . . . (also 8:55).
   3:20f.—Every one who does evil—But he who does
       what is true. . . .

3:31ff.—He who comes from above is above all—He who is of the earth speaks of the earth.

3:36—He who believes . . . has eternal life—He who does not believe, the wrath of God rests upon him.

6:36—"You have seen me and yet do not believe."

8:21f.—"I go away, and you will . . . die in your sin" (28f.).

8:23f.—"You are from below, I am from above."

8:55—"You have not known him; I know him."

1.1 One group establishes its contrasting origin

8:33–36—You are not free, you are slaves to sin.

8:37–39—"I speak of what I have seen with my Father, and you do what you have heard from your father."

8:40–44—You do the works of your father, the devil.

8:45–47—You do not believe me because you are not of God.

8:55—"You have not known him; I know him."

2. The bread of life providing eternal life (spiritualism)

6:47–51a—I am the true bread, unlike the manna.

6:51b–56—The flesh is like the bread.

8:51–58—Eternal life, immortality are promised (as in 5:24); Abraham and Jesus live eternally.

3. Judgment

3:18f.—The judgment is construed as ahistorical.

12:30f.—Now is the judgment; the believer is already judged.

12:31—Jesus' death and the judgment of the world occur simultaneously.

5:25—"The hour is coming, and now is."

4. Devaluation of creatureliness, of the manna, and of the multiplication of the loaves.

5. The stylistic form of intensification and emphasis, for example, 5:20b: "greater works than these will [the Father] show him."

6. Immortality, the true bread, the true light.

Unclassified motifs

1. Neutral concepts

   The term "believe" occurs in the earlier and in the later layer, for example, 6:29: "that you believe in him whom he has sent."

   The negative use of "But . . . you do not believe" is akin to establishing a contrast.

   "Truth" and "lie" (8:44–47) are generally used in the abstract, for example, 14:6: "I am the . . . truth."

2. Unclassified sayings

   3:33—"he who receives his testimony sets his seal to this, that God is true."

   3:34—"He whom God has sent utters the words of God."

   4:35f.—Comparison with the harvest (4:38: commissioning the disciples).

   12:24–26—The grain of wheat has to fall into the earth.

   12:44–50—Variations of the "light of the world" motif, linked with other motifs.

3. Individual sayings rejecting the establishment of a contrast (origin questionable)

   3:16f.—"For God so loved the world that . . . whoever believes in him should not perish."

   12:47—"I did not come to judge the world but to save the world."

It is important to note that, apart from the later layer, individual gnostic motifs or sayings occur only in additions to discourses. Old Testament parallels, however, occur in great number and variety in the entire Gospel.

Integrating the Controversy Dialogues into the Gospel

Common to the five controversy dialogues is the occurrence in each of a dialogue between "Jesus" and the "Jews." From beginning to end, all five of them contain only this dialogue between the same parties.

Something similar can be seen in the controversy dialogue between Job and his friends. In both cases there
is an underlying story (in Job it is the framework). The
controversy dialogue is inserted into this story and
assists its interpretation.

Of the five controversy dialogues, only the third
(7:14–36) is part of the narrative of Jesus of Nazareth.
John 7:14 begins with a time reference, and the continuation in 7:37 likewise contains a reference to time. It is
a genuine forensic controversy. It is entirely part of the
earlier layer.

The two controversy dialogues that precede it (5:17–
47 and 6:25–65) do not fit organically. Although there
is no preceding discourse, 5:17 begins with the statement "But Jesus answered them. . . . " In the second
controversy dialogue (6:25ff.), the Jews initially ask
Jesus, "Rabbi, when did you come here?" Thereupon,
Jesus' discourse begins abruptly, "Jesus answered them
. . . ," though it is not a response to the Jews' question.
In the case of both these controversy dialogues, it can
safely be said that they were inserted subsequently.

The fourth controversy dialogue begins without a
concrete situation after 8:11 (i.e., 7:52): "Again Jesus
spoke to them, saying. . . . "

The fifth dialogue follows the time reference in
10:22. It is introduced in v. 24: "So the Jews gathered
round him" with the intention of getting him to say
whether he is the Christ. Jesus' discourse does not
address a messianic claim. The insertion of the dialogue
at this juncture is made necessary by 10:27f., a citation
from the shepherd discourse.

On the basis of these findings, it appears that, as far
as its form and content are concerned, only the third
controversy dialogue was a component of the Gospel
from the start. The others were inserted later. All of
them, however, belong together to the extent that they
share the same form and the same parties are speaking.
They have been inserted en bloc.

4

The Significance of the Old Testament for the Gospel of John

1. The issue is not whether the writer of the Gospel knows the Old Testament, nor whether or not and how often Old Testament sayings occur in it. Rather, the issue is whether there is a commonality between the Gospel and the Old Testament in how they speak about God, the world, and human beings. In other words: Is the God whom Jesus calls "my Father" the same as the one of whom the Old Testament speaks? If someone praying in the Psalms says to this God, "You are our refuge," does it refer to the same God of whom Jesus says, "I and the Father are one"? And when he says, "My Father is working still," does it denote the work of which the Old Testament speaks?

2. The Old Testament narrates a history; the Gospel of John narrates part of the history. The Old Testament begins with creation; at its beginning, the Gospel of John refers to creation. The Gospel of John narrates a part of the history, beginning with Jesus' ministry and ending with his death. From beginning to end, he is taking a path characterized by travel references, like

those in the Old Testament associated with segments of history, especially that of the journey through the wilderness after the liberation from Egypt. What Jesus did, said, and suffered are events on this journey (except for the controversy dialogues that lack the travel references).

3. The atmosphere of the events and discourses of Jesus on this journey is an altogether Old Testament one. Why should it be any different if it takes place in the land of the patriarchs, if the history of the patriarchs is still alive, as shown especially in the conversation with the Samaritan woman! There are no traces at all of foreign, gnostic thought penetrating this atmosphere. During the time of his ministry, Jesus' journey took him through the countryside and into smaller country towns; apart from Jerusalem, he did not come into contact with larger towns. In the country and in country towns, it is hardly possible for philosophical speculations to develop. It is the natural thing that the people with whom Jesus conversed and among whom he ministered lived and thought in keeping with the thinking of the patriarchs, as we know it from the Old Testament.

4. It is this atmosphere that helps the understanding of what Jesus says concerning his relationship with the Father. In this lies the key to the history of Jesus of Nazareth: "My Father is working still, and I am working" (5:17). Jesus is sent from God, his Father. Without God he can do nothing; he wants only to do the Father's will. He is as much aware of being sent as were the prophets before him, as described by the commissioning narratives. The story of Jesus follows the story of the prophets. God sent him to the same people and into the same country as he sent them, and he speaks the same language they did. The history of this people is presupposed in his mission, together with their tradition, the Scriptures.

Everything involved in the motif of Jesus' relationship with God is included here. Jesus works in agreement with the Father and his works. He wants only to do the Father's will, not his own: He does not seek his own glory but only that of the Father. All of this can be said in precisely the same way of the prophets. Like the prophets, Jesus was called when he was a grown man, and as was true of the prophets, the time of his ministry was limited.

Like the prophets, he spoke what he had to say in the name of God, without orders from human beings or from an institution. Thus, what he said and did was controversial and open to attack. Like the prophets, he was helpless, and like them he suffered.

The tidings of Jesus, like the tidings of the prophets, were preserved and handed down in *the form of a history*, that is, a segment of history. In the earliest phase, this could only have been an oral tradition. Neither the tradition of the prophets nor that of Jesus had the form of a doctrine, of a systematic presentation. The tidings arose from individual scenes in which the prophets and Jesus spoke and acted.

It has been observed frequently that the affinity between the Gospel of John and *the prophet Jeremiah* is particularly close. Both had been called and sent by God; the ministry of each ends in suffering, which in both cases gave rise to their significance for the future. The history of Jesus has its prehistory in the prophetic history and thereby is also directly linked with the history of Israel (cf. pp. 5–6 for Isaiah's vision of commissioning).

Furthermore, the Gospel of John has close affinities with *Deutero-Isaiah*. The association of Isaiah 52–53 with Jesus' passion in the New Testament is commonly acknowledged. Beyond the fact that a passion story is the goal in both instances, they also agree in their understanding of the work of God. While Isaiah 40–53 deals with the redemptive work of God, his beneficent work is added in chs. 54–55. The same is true in the Gospel of John. Whereas chs. 1–12 address the Savior's redemptive work, chs. 13–17, the farewell discourses, present his beneficent work by means of the key word "abiding," especially as depicted in the parable of the Vine and the Branches in ch. 15. For this reason, the Gospel of John is misjudged if the redemptive work of Christ is construed as encompassing merely his death and resurrection. He is the Christ who helps, heals, and blesses, for whom precisely this kind of ministry brought on his suffering. He is the good shepherd who suffered: "The good shepherd lays down his life for the sheep" (10:11). Perhaps this statement expresses most clearly that the redemptive work of Jesus cannot be restricted to his death and resurrection, for in this comparison his death is brought about precisely by his support of the endangered ones among the sheep he tends as the shepherd. This can refer only to the ministry in Jesus' life.

5. In the Old Testament, the personal suffering of individual human beings plays a major part; as sufferers, they are taken seriously, together with their experiences of suffering. For this reason, it is not merely the laments of individuals that are part of the Bible, in such books as Job, the Psalms, and Lamentations; human suffering is also encountered time and again in a host of narratives, from the earliest times to the most recent. Taking seriously the suffering of individuals is precisely what belongs to the milieu of the Gospel of John. Jesus initiates his discourses with conversations with individuals: Conversations with those who suffer or with their loved ones are always part of the healing narratives (ch. 11). In each case, Jesus attends to the *individual* sufferer. This is one of the major features the Old Testament and the Gospel of John hold in common, though this has been virtually ignored until now. The transition from lament to praise has found a significant echo in the ministry of the Savior, the healer. When Jesus perceives the works of God in the healings he

performs, it is evident that it is the same God who in the Old Testament transforms the laments of the sufferers into praise.

6. Jesus' proclamation also links him with the prophets. He does not want to proclaim his own teaching, a Jesus doctrine; what he has to say he hears from his Father (7:16). This agrees with the language of the prophetic declarations, which are introduced with: "Thus says (has said) Yahweh." Jesus does not defend a theology or even a Christology of his own. He is proclaiming the words of God, not the words of Jesus. Hence, they cannot contradict what God has said in the Old Testament!

This is particularly apparent in the I-am sayings as a focused example of Jesus' proclamation. They are individual sayings from the oral tradition, all of which are comparisons in accordance with the parables of Jesus in the other Gospels. All of them are sayings that promise salvation and offer an invitation to this salvation: "If any one thirst, let him come to me and drink" (7:37). In this regard, they are in contrast with the motif of the later layer of the controversy dialogues, namely, the stating of a contrast that rejects and condemns. All of the comparative features are part of creation, of what has been made, of everyday, this-worldly life. This is the kind of comparison Jesus draws concerning his ministry when he says, "My Father is working still, and I am working" (5:17). His deeds and words remain in the realm of the created, in contrast to dualistic teaching, which has little regard for the created and recognizes only spiritual reality: "the flesh is of no avail" (6:63).

7. There is frequent mention of the Scriptures as the vehicle of the tradition of the Jewish people, and they are not a matter of dispute between Jesus and his opponents; both refer to them. In this context, the relationship between the Gospel of John and the Old Testament is self-evident. Jesus appeals to the Scriptures, for they

bear witness to him. Certainly that also includes the texts that announce the coming of the Messiah. More important, however, is that the Scriptures affirm the work of God right up to the present, to his being sent. In the Scriptures, Jesus found God's work in all its fullness, the work of the creator, of the beneficent God, of the one who directs the fortunes of human beings, of the one who also "[gives] to the young ravens [their food]" (Ps 147:9). What are meant here especially are the psalms of praise, which laud the work of God in all its fullness.

In a number of instances Jesus levels an open and self-threatening criticism of the Jewish use of the law, though not at the Scriptures per se. Thus he states several times that the stern preachers of the law themselves do not always thoroughly adhere to it. They condemn Jesus for healing on the Sabbath while they themselves circumcise on the Sabbath. They dare not cast the first stone against the woman caught in adultery. Nicodemus objects that the law does not condemn anyone without first having given him a hearing. The leaders curse the common people who do not know the law. In the face of such abuse, however, Jesus affirms the Scriptures and holds them in high esteem.

8. The events that transpired on Jesus' journey should be distinguished from the interpretation of his deeds and words. This includes the texts that reproduce, from start to finish, the effect of what Jesus says and does, to the extent that these texts presuppose an interpretation. This is also true of various kinds of discourse elements in which Jesus himself interprets what he says and does, as in the saying "I am the good shepherd," where he provides the interpretation in the statements that follow it.

The distinction between interpretation and event (words and deeds) is of fundamental importance for understanding the Gospel. This has become clear to me from the historical books of the Old Testament. Understanding them is indeed made possible only by means of this distinction. The book of Joshua, for instance, consists mainly of interpretation. This happens especially in discourses, in the Gospel of John as well as in Joshua (chs. 1, 23, 24); hence, there is agreement here also. Concerning this correspondence, it is particularly important for understanding the Gospel of John not only to distinguish between interpretation and event but also to determine the types and forms of interpretation. From this it becomes apparent that discourses, as they occur in the controversy dialogues, are fundamentally different from discourses in which Jesus explains the comparison with the shepherd, or from conversations in which Jesus speaks with an individual, for instance, the woman of Samaria.

9. In conclusion, mention must be made of another important commonality. In the Gospel of John, a major role is given to the conversation, especially to the dialogue. This becomes clear from the fact that the two initial speech elements in the Gospel are dialogues: with Nicodemus and with the Samaritan woman. The peculiarity of these conversations is that Jesus' answers are often mysterious; they are intended to stimulate reflection. This occurs only in the Gospel of John. The importance of the conversation has its origin in the Old Testament, where it indeed has a similarly large significance in all sections. One may recall "Abraham and Isaac on the way" or the conversations in the narratives of the succession to the throne, for a conversation is an event, a necessary part of many stories.

The interpreter of the Gospel of John who does not see the significance of the conversations in this Gospel cannot understand it. It is no accident that especially the very abstract explanations have no awareness of, and nothing to say about, the conversations. This in turn is linked with the fact that the gnostic motifs in the Gospel of John do not recognize conversation. The only thing they know is the controversy dialogue, where conversation does not occur.

This again is predicated upon the most important difference between the two layers. Every conversation is a process, an event in time. The difference between the earlier and the later layers is especially that the former speaks historically while the latter speaks ahistorically. This distinction can be supported with overwhelming evidence. Hence, the roots of the earlier layer and of the remainder of the Gospel are in the Old Testament; conversely, those of the later layer are in a conception of reality that is entirely ahistorical.

10. There is only one component of the Gospel of John that is in contrast with the Old Testament: the motifs of gnostic and spiritual dualism, the roots of which are not found in the Old Testament. They are restricted to the later layer in the controversy dialogues. It is the intention of the "Jesus" speaking in this layer (he cannot be Jesus of Nazareth) to dissociate himself from the "Jews" (they are not the Jews of history), whom he perceives as opponents. The thinking of this layer is ahistorical and speculative. It is the thinking of a group contrasted with the Old Testament. In this layer there emerges a view of the human being and the world in which these are not creatures and the Old Testament understanding of creation is fundamentally negated. This rejection of creator and creation (cf. pp. 45f.) does not agree with the rest of the Gospel, which begins with creation. What is apparent here is gnostic influence; the negation of creation is a sure criterion for this.

This is in keeping with a gnostic understanding of reality contrasted with that of the Old Testament. History does not exist within it. It is replaced by a structure conversant with only two opposing world systems: one determined from below, the other from above; one is characterized as heavenly, the other as earthly/worldly. They are two spiritual realms, for which there is neither time nor history; both of them are timeless.

From what has been said, it follows that the Old Testament provides unequivocal criteria that make it possible to differentiate between biblical and gnostic motifs in the controversy dialogues (cf. pp. 27f.) At the same time, it becomes clear that the earlier layer of the controversy dialogues in all essentials agrees with the remainder of the Gospel and that the gnostic influence is almost entirely confined to the later layer of the controversy dialogues.

Along with this, the later layer has a devaluation of the Old Testament and of its account of history. The origin of the present generation from Abraham is merely "fleshly" and, as such, is not significant. Those addressed in ch. 8 are not descendants of Abraham, nor are they God's creatures; their father is the devil. The miracle of the manna in the wilderness wanderings is devalued because the manna did not render them immortal; those who ate of it died. It was not the real bread because it did not convey immortality. The same applies to the miracle of the multiplication of the loaves, for it did not effect immortality: "Do not labor for the food which perishes" (6:27). Both devalue the creator and the creation. As with the bread, so the flesh that is to be eaten in order to attain immortality is removed from the act of Jesus' Last Supper and is designated to become the means for attaining immortality. Human creatureliness within the boundaries of birth and death is denied; Abraham and Jesus live eternally. Resurrection is replaced with immortality of the soul. Jesus is preexistent; his earthly birth is meaningless.

All of this one encounters only in the later layer of the controversy dialogues, not in the rest of the Gospel. The contrast between the view of reality expressed in the former and that of the Gospel, in agreement with the Old Testament, is evident. The contrast with the Old Testament is the decisive criterion in distinguishing between gnostic motifs and those of the Gospel.

5

Conclusions

The Gospel of John and Paul

In the earlier layer of the controversy dialogues, the ministry and words of Jesus in his earthly life are important, and to this extent this layer agrees with the rest of the Gospel. Jesus' earthly ministry bears witness to him; it witnesses to his oneness with the Father, who shows him "all things."

In the later layer of the controversy dialogues, the ministry of Jesus in his earthly life is unimportant; it is not presented at all. For Jesus and for faith in him, all that matters is his heavenly origin ("I am from above") and that he will be exalted again to his heavenly existence ("when I am lifted up"). Redemption takes place exclusively by means of an exaltation, that is, by means of his death and resurrection. What he said and did in his earthly life is without significance in the later layer.

This is quite similar to Paul, for whom Jesus' work and words on earth have little significance, if any at all: "we regard [Christ from a human point of view] no longer" (2 Cor. 5:16). In this regard, Paul is closer to the later gnostic layer of the controversy dialogues than to the rest of the Gospel of John. Paul is also closer to this later, gnostic layer than to the rest of the Gospel in another respect. In this later layer, the issue is a state of being, that is, two contrasting states of being. Something similar is true of Paul. (On this see C. Westermann, "Zur Sprachstruktur des Römerbriefes" [On the linguistic structure of Romans], in *"In Dubio pro Deo": Heidelberger Resonanzen auf den 50. Geburtstag von G. Theissen* [ed. D. Trobisch; 1993] 351–363.) The intensifications in the description of this state of being (e.g., 2 Cor. 5:17) occur in Paul as well. Accordingly, static, ahistorical thinking is dominant in Paul as well as in the later layer.

Jesus the Messiah

Only once do the Jews ask whether Jesus is the Messiah, and Jesus responds evasively (10:24f.). The entry into Jerusalem, in which Jesus is hailed as the king, is common to the Gospel of John and the Synoptics, but it is provided a different meaning by the symbolic act of footwashing that follows. Even the anointing at Bethany was not a royal anointing. Otherwise there are no extant royal features; neither is the shepherd in ch. 10 reminiscent of a king.

Only the passion narrative states that Jesus was condemned and executed as a king. The Gospel of John does not have any "messianic prophecies." Especially in the controversy dialogues, there is no reference to a king, although the dispute about whether Jesus was the promised Messiah would have made good sense there.

The Gospel of John must be in line with a tradition in which there was no reference to Jesus as the fulfillment of a messianic promise. This is comprehensible, inasmuch as the later layer of the controversy dialogues cannot have been interested in it, since its thinking is gnostic-philosophical and entirely ahistorical.

It is all the more important that, in the earlier layer of the controversy dialogues, Jesus was clearly seen in line with the prophets. This has been argued earlier (cf.

pp. 65f.) Therefore the designation "Jesus as king" (Christ), which emerged after Jesus' death and continues to this day, is at least one-sided. But it can also be said that it has become merely a name in which the actual meaning is no longer recalled.

This name touches upon the divisive question between Jews and Christians of whether Jesus is the Messiah, or whether the Messiah has not yet come. From the Christian perspective, too, it is necessary to acknowledge that the Messiah who was expected among the Jewish people then, namely, a royal figure with a royal claim, is not personified in Jesus of Nazareth, for his life and ministry, his suffering and death, are entirely in line with the prophets and the prophetic tradition. This, in any case, is true in the Gospel of John. As an introduction to the farewell discourses, the footwashing, too, shows that Jesus is in line with the "servant" in Isaiah 52–53 and not in line with a king of the time of redemption. If it is taken into consideration that Jesus of Nazareth belongs to the line of the prophetic traditions of Israel, the contentious question between Jews and Christians can at least be defused.

It is also important to remember that, in the Gospel of John, neither the concept of redemption nor the verb "to redeem" occurs until John 17. When the Father sends Jesus, it is not stated that he is sent to redeem Israel or all people. What is stated is that he is sent to do the Father's work. What this work entails, or what the message that he is to bring to human beings consists of, is not stated explicitly. It is to be derived indirectly from Jesus' words and deeds. It is particularly conspicuous that any reference to sin and forgiveness of sins is, at best, peripheral. Until John 17, *Jesus' ministry* is expressed in healing the sick and in saving people from trouble and distress. His *speaking* is determined by the fact that he himself is the Savior who invites all to salvation, which he is able to give. This is expressed with particular clarity in the I-am sayings and in the comparisons.

Closing Remarks

At the end of this study, the question must be asked, In which direction does its result point? If the Old Testament is assumed to have substantial influence upon the Gospel of John, how would the scholarly inquiry have to proceed?

If this assumption is granted, the continuation follows naturally: The components of this "account" would have to be identified and examined individually. For instance, the texts that have been summarily designated as discourses would have to be investigated for their characteristics, and the dialogues recognized in terms of their own significance. The character of the whole document is shown only from a composite perspective of all of its parts as parts of the whole.

The Gospel of John is often still described as a narrative, and its "narratival character" is attributed special significance. It is not a narrative, however, and has no narratival character. (The designation "narratival" is used all too frequently and too hastily today.) It is important to differentiate between narrative and account; this applies to the entire New Testament, as well as to the Old Testament. In my opinion, however, a clear and precise distinction between the two is possible only by bringing into play the Old Testament, because the number of texts from which criteria for differentiating can be drawn is much larger and the forms themselves emerge more clearly.

This is one of the areas where isolating New Testament research from that of the Old Testament can no longer be justified. There are indeed texts in the Gospel of John that contain narratival features or that come close to a narrative; but the Gospel as a whole is an account. (On distinguishing between narrative and account, cf. C. Westermann, *Die Geschichtsbücher des Alten Testaments: Gab es ein deuteronomistisches Geschichtswerk?* [Gütersloh: Kaiser, 1994]).

The individual components, as parts of the whole, partly form groups of texts of symmetrical or similar structure. These groups form the context of the individual texts (as in Bultmann, *History of the Synoptic Tradition,* 1963), for instance, the healing accounts or the I-am sayings (so H. Thyen; see pp. 100–101 below). A composite perspective of the entire Gospel can be gained only if the components themselves can be assessed as totalities.

The most widely held opinion today, that the text of the Gospel is homogenous (reinforced even more by asserting a synchronic origin), is to no avail at all if one does not explain at the same time how ahistorical motifs relate to those that are historically orientated, or what the relationship is between the words of Jesus' inviting, open proclamation and the statements that set up boundaries, that reject and condemn.

Jesus' extremely anti-Semitic sayings ("You are of your father the devil"), which contravene everything we know otherwise about Jesus, are a particular problem for the assertion of homogeneity.

Recently it has been argued very emphatically that the Gospel of John is a book like others, namely, literature for reading purposes. First of all, this cannot be the case for this reason: Literature is noncommittal, but this is not true of the Gospel of John (20:31). The Gospel's origin can be explained only on the basis of the awareness that it is not noncommittal. As an end product, it is a writing by and for interested persons, and it originated as such. What interested people in this writing was Jesus and faith in Jesus (20:31). The same is true for the intention from which it originated. From the start, that is, beginning with the death of Jesus, it was a group interest that was continually kept alive, first with the disciples and then also with the subsequent generations.

In its simplest form, this interest appears in the inquiry about Jesus after his death. A woman joining the community, a man joining the community first questioned those who had been there from the beginning. They inquired into his ministry, his deeds and his words. In this connection, the travel references took on importance ("Did he also come to this place?"). This means that in the beginning the tradition was oral; there was no other way. When those who had newly joined the community asked about Jesus and an eyewitness answered, there was no Gospel to cite; the only thing he or she could do was repeat individual events or brief sayings or brief groups of sayings. This can still be seen in the form of the Gospels handed down to us. They confirm that the small units were there at the beginning because they were handed down orally. It is difficult to comprehend that scholars today still deny this early oral stage of the tradition, without being able to provide another explanation. In this context, too, the backdrop of the Old Testament is important.

The special characteristic of the Gospels, including John, is that they are *living writings*. By this I mean that they are writings that evolved, and their development was necessitated by the history of the community, alive with interest in the content of these writings, the Gospels: the life and ministry of Jesus. It is highly unlikely that the Gospel of John originated as the work of a man of letters, apart from a relationship with this community and merely for the purpose of reading.

The Gospel of John is also a dynamic writing in the sense that some of its components had a life of their own before they were integrated into this writing. In the first instance, this applies to the healing narratives, which are closely related to those found in the first three Gospels and cannot be understood apart from

them and from their history; neither are they comprehensible apart from the healing narratives in the Old
Testament. The same applies to such fixed forms as the
accounts, travel references, and the like.

The fact that the Gospel of John contains components with genres that also occur in other parts of the
Bible prohibits an interpretation that insists upon their
"synchronic" origin.

Finally, the Gospel of John is also a living writing
because a diachronic origin is certain in some instances.
If the epilogue of ch. 21 was added to chs. 1–20 of the
Gospel, this is basically not a literary procedure but a
procedure of the community in which the Gospel originated. It presupposes that the Gospel was read and
studied and that members of the community considered
this supplement essential.

The additions of 5:25 and 28 can be explained only
by the assertion that there were some in the community
in which the Gospel of John was read and studied who
objected to what the text said about the end times. They
inserted their dissent in the text. Similar things can be
observed in a few other instances.

Differences between the Gospel of John and the three
earlier Gospels may indicate changes in the community.
If exorcisms are completely absent from the healing
accounts in the Gospel of John, this is not the decision
of a writer. Rather, this signals a change in the community of those who believed in Jesus. For them, exorcisms
had in the meantime largely lost their significance.

Thus, it is precisely the variety of voices that renders the Gospel of John a living writing. The same
variety can already be seen in the first generation after
Jesus, in the New Testament letters.

I have stated that the atmosphere of the Old Testament can be seen in the Gospel of John. This could be
developed further. But there is also much here that can
only be sensed. Only if one has been immersed in this

atmosphere for a long time does one begin to grasp how, in their fullness and wealth, the parts of the Old Testament form a totality. In the final analysis, I abide by the assertion that the Gospel of John cannot be understood without considering this background.

Another perspective needs to be addressed here. Only those who know the Old Testament and who see it in the background of the Gospel of John can see the boundaries of the latter. The Gospel can at best present only a very small excerpt of what God is and what God does. That he is the creator is merely intimated at the beginning and remains undeveloped.

If one considers that the story of Jesus of Nazareth is only an extract of God's universal work and that the lordship of God over history is merely touched on, and if one remembers what the Old Testament psalms of praise had to say of the work of this God, only then does one recognize this narrow extract of his work, which can be grasped properly only against the backdrop of the comprehensive work of God. It is not appropriate to treat the extract as the totality. Likewise, what the account of the Gospel of John recounts of the ministry and words of Jesus can be only an extract. The Gospel is not the Bible. Only from the perspective of the Bible as a whole does it take on importance and meaning.

Epilogue

Examples of Recent Interpretations:
A Contribution to the History of Research

Rudolf Bultmann, "Johannesevangelium" ["Gospel of John"], *Die Religion in Geschichte und Gegenwart* (3d ed.; 6 vols.; Tübingen: Mohr Siebeck, 1957–1962), 3.840–50.

Concerning the literary character of the Gospel, Bultmann first says that, since the order of the texts is frequently disturbed, the Gospel of John must be the result of redaction. He assumes that it originated essentially from three sources: a collection of miracle stories, another of revelation discourses, and a third of passion and resurrection stories (3.842f.).

Bultmann's assumption has been discussed intensively and rejected by many scholars. Because of the indication of a numbering (John 2:11) and the similarity to the miracle stories in the Synoptic Gospels, a collection of miracle stories available to the evangelist is plausible. Conversely, a collection of discourses is unlikely because of their diversity. That the discourses are constructed in keeping with a schema applies only to the group of I-am sayings (six or seven texts), to nothing else. Most interpreters use the designation "discourses" far too broadly; the Gospel contains no discourses along the lines of rhetoric. Jesus offers no speeches from a podium or from a pulpit. He is on a par with his audience and is exposed to any objection or contradiction. At the least, dialogues (chs. 3 and 4) must be distinguished from discourses. The controversy dialogues in chs. 5–10 (except 9) are very different from the parabolic discourses in chs. 10 and 15.

Bultmann explained the difference from the Synoptics as follows: While the latter are composed of loosely attached individual texts, the author of the Gospel of John formed the material into a thematically determined unit.

The Gospel of John, however, does not consist of "materials" organized by themes; it is not didactic literature. Rather, the difference is that the evangelist formed a coherent account out of individual pieces, such as a healing, especially by connecting them with conversations. Most interpreters have not noted this distinction, that the Gospel of John is an account (not a narrative!) in which the travel references are the basic framework pointing the way from the beginning to the end of Jesus' ministry. It is structured in keeping with the stations of this journey, not according to themes but a sequence of events. This is already hinted at in vv. 11–12 of the prologue: "He came to his own home" (chs. 1–6); "his own people received him not" (chs. 7–12); "But to all who received him . . ." (chs. 13–17). This comprehensive formation, too, is structured as an account whose focus is on the passion.

The discourses and conversations are likewise not a treatment of a topic but, rather, primarily something that takes place between the parties involved. Bultmann's notion that all of the discourses have essentially one theme only, namely, the person of Jesus as the revealer, indicates again that he perceived the Gospel as timeless. Jesus is not a theme. In each discourse, the issue is an event, and in each discourse, in keeping with his journey, it is a different event. Why should Jesus be sent from the Father to address the same theme time and again?

For Bultmann, chs. 10 and 15 are pictorial discourses or symbolic discourses. Pictures and symbols, however, represent things that already exist. In contrast, Jesus speaks of interactions that have happened or will happen. For example, something happens between the shepherd and those he tends. Something else happens to the vine and the branches (analogous to God's saving and beneficent work; cf. pp. 64–65).

Bultmann's most frequently discussed thesis is that "John's language originates from a gnostic dualism," an assertion he develops further. This is certainly accurate in the case of a statement such as "You are from below, I am from above" (8:23) and of many similar contrasts. Moreover, there is a whole series of statements in which a gnostic origin can be seen. They are often in stark contrast to other statements in the Gospel of John. This is also the case when Bultmann describes the basic features of the gnostic redeemer myth (3.847) and then continues, "It is in the language of this mythology that the Gospel of John describes the ministry of Jesus as revelation." This applies to parts of the Gospel of John but by no means to the whole Gospel. It applies mainly to the controversy dialogues between Jesus and the Jews (Bultmann's comment is apt: "In the Gospel of John, the Jews are the representatives of the unbelievers"). But these dialogues are to be divided into an earlier and a later layer: In the earlier layer the language is that of the Gospel, while in the later one it is influenced by gnostic dualism (cf. pp. 24f., 27f.). In the later layer, a heavenly being descends from heaven to earth; in the earlier, the Son is sent to people from the Father. This sending of the Son by the Father corresponds with the sending of the prophets at an earlier time (cf. pp. 26f.). The features mentioned in the Gospel of John in this context correspond with those of the sending of the prophets (with particular clarity in Jeremiah). Like Bultmann, most interpreters have never even considered this parallel.

In Bultmann's concluding statements (3.847f.), his position becomes particularly clear: "Gnosticism . . . construed God's nonworldliness in radical terms and likewise also the conception of redemption and revelation. . . . The Gospel of John appropriates this tradition. . . . *The idea of revelation* is construed in radical terms here." Thus Bultmann clearly argues that, for him, Gnosticism is a product of the imagination. When he concludes that the Gospel of John appropriates this tradition, he characterizes the Gospel of John as an idea; hence, the Gospel would also be a product of mental creation. But the Gospel of John reports events; it has the structure of a narrative. In John, revelation is not the product of imagination; it is what happens. This cannot be denied in the face of the consistent verbal structure. The first sentence that speaks of Jesus, that is, of the revealer, is a verbal sentence (1:14). The Gospel of John deals not with concepts of revelation but with its historical fact and with how it occurs in the history that is reported in the Gospel. The healings Jesus performed (and which do not occur in Gnostic myths!) are events, even if they are interpreted as signs. When one of those who were healed says, "one thing I know, that though I was blind, now I see" (9:25), he speaks of an event that took place.

The Gospel of John cannot be understood apart from the Old Testament. The Old Testament relates a history. This history continues in the New Testament; this is what the Gospels report. When the history of Jesus, like that of Jeremiah, ends in a passion account, both speak of events that happened.

Bultmann's formulation that "Gnosticism . . . construed God's nonworldliness [I would say removal from the world] in radical terms" is suspicious. If God is radically nonworldly, he cannot be its creator.

Bultmann assumes that the order of the texts is frequently disturbed. All interpreters today agree on this, even if they, like H. Thyen, attribute only minor significance to such disruptions. Bultmann uses these disruptions to conclude that, "for this reason, the Gospel of John must be the result of redaction." Since "redaction" is generally understood as a procedure encompassing the work as a whole, this theory is given too much weight; against this it can be argued that the Gospel of John originated "synchronically" as the work of one author (so H. Thyen). It is therefore appropriate simply to speak of a process taking a longer period of time, hence, of many who were working on the text and in very different ways. Thus, the correction of the end-time discourse in 5:25, for instance, is altogether different from adding the concept of "flesh" in 6:51b–56 to that of "bread." These two are independent corrections, additions, or changes, but they are not the work of a single redactor.

In this connection, it should be assumed that the long period between the events associated with Jesus of Nazareth, around the year 30, and the origin of the Gospel of John in the form we have, around the turn of the first into the second century, passed uneventfully. The Gospel of John is an account, and an account always must originate from facts. That the interim passed uneventfully is impossible, first of all because the original tradition of the deeds and words of Jesus was oral—and no one contests that—and there must be a path from the oral to the written tradition. This path led from the initial writing, via summaries or collections, all the way to the Synoptic Gospels and, beyond them, to the Fourth Gospel. In this connection, it is generally ignored that the oral tradition initially consisted of small units only, and that longer discourses, as well as collections of individual sayings, such as the Sermon on the Mount, represent a later phase. The evangelists' own reworkings were then added. The conversations of Jesus, as in John 3 and 4, are certainly the work of the evangelist. The same does not apply, however, to sayings in which the early form of the logia (individual sayings) can still be recognized, as in the I-am sayings. In the case of the latter, it is plausible that they originated in the oral tradition.

The assertion of many interpreters, however, that the Fourth Gospel originated *only* in a synchronic way and *only* from a single author is merely hypothetical. Most of the time one fails to remember that the continuity of the account about Jesus, beginning with the oral tradition of the early period, is certified by the existence and continuity of the Christian communities, all of which, in every generation, wanted to hear and know something about Jesus.

It is equally certain that in the Synoptics these early traditions were varied and multiform. Many of the breaks and discontinuities can be explained by the many coexisting and parallel traditions. They posed particular problems for the Fourth Gospel because the evangelist aspired to a coherent presentation of the ministry of Jesus. The case of the first three Gospels is different because, apart from the passion, they allowed the small units that were handed down to remain such by stringing them together.

Ernst Käsemann, *The Testament of Jesus: A Study of the Gospel of John in the Light of Chapter 17* (ET; Philadelphia: Fortress, 1968).

Käsemann begins with the historical formulation of the question:

"Historically, the Gospel as a whole remains an enigma, in spite of the elucidation of individual details" (p. 2). Yet Käsemann's agenda is dogmatic: "The Johannine eschatology will be treated under the aspects of Christology, ecclesiology, and soteriology" (p. 3). No explanation is offered, however, for this mixing and interweaving of a historical and, at the same time, dogmatic study. His chapter titles (The Glory of Christ; The Community under the Word; Christian Unity) are ample indication that he was not concerned more with dogmatic than with historical issues. Käsemann must be asked the following question: The Gospel of John is an account. If John renders an account of Jesus' ministry from start to finish, on what methodological grounds does Käsemann deal with this account in a dogmatic study?

If Käsemann were to proceed exegetically, he would state first of all what he means by "glory." This term can take on very different meanings. Käsemann's own understanding of it cannot be ascertained from his study. In order to do this, he would have to provide the structure of ch. 17. This is absolutely essential in a chapter as complex as this. For Käsemann, it is sufficient to cull out a few themes. Concerning its form, he argues that it makes use of the structure of a farewell discourse of one who is dying. This does apply to chs. 14–16 but not to ch. 17. Then he suggests that John 17 is composed as a prayer, then that is a piece of instruction. Evidently the form is not important for him.

"Glorification" is a key term. It is already made manifest and, at the same time, still to come; it is present and future eschatology at the same time (p. 9ff.). This is a dogmatic assertion; an exegete would not state that a statement is at once present and future. The believer has already moved from death to life. Earthly death is meaningless where Jesus appears. The hour of the passion is synonymous with the hour of the glorification. In Christ the end of the world remains present. Käsemann is correct in saying that all of these statements are clearly gnostic. For Gnosticism, time, as a course of time, does not exist, nor does history. Käsemann does not succeed, however, in maintaining this blending of present and future consistently throughout the Gospel. On p. 70 he says, "On the basis of his presuppositions John developed something like a unique futurist eschatology and John 17 indicates that the Evangelist not only focussed his attention upon the past and present but that he also possessed a future hope." When he argues at the beginning (p. 3) that ch. 17 represents a summary of the Johannine discourses but that precisely this chapter contains an eschatology of the future, this does not bode well for Käsemann's argument. This circumstance demonstrates that the Gospel of John is not as uniformly gnostic as Käsemann would have it. The same applies when he describes the Gospel of John as the "message of God who walks on the face of the earth" (p. 66); while he agrees that the statement that God sent his Son into the world is something quite different, he nevertheless seeks to tone down the meaning of this statement (pp. 12–13). When he describes the phrase "the Father who sent me" as a "christological formula" (p. 11), this is incorrect. It is the report of an event. It is concerned with something that happened, not with a state of being. The same is true when Käsemann contrasts this phrase with the other: "I and the Father are one." As the context bears out, the issue is Jesus' oneness with the Father in his work on earth.

Käsemann rejects a "Christology of humiliation" and plays down the significance of the statement "The Word became flesh and dwelt among us" in the prologue (pp. 9–10); Jesus is "the Christ who walks on the face of the earth"; he is "God, descending into the human realm" (p. 13). This description is not objective but tendentious, since for Käsemann Jesus' earthly ministry is meaningless and "in the realm of deficiencies and defects" (p. 34). It cannot have any meaning because it is presented in the Gospel as a history, and there is no history in gnostic thought; "the characteristic feature of this world cannot be a history which arranges the world's epochs and signifies its immanent path" (p. 34). "The Johannine salvation history is, to be precise, in its very essence the history of the Logos" (p. 35). In Käsemann's work, there is not a single reference to Jesus speaking with a human being. But if the major part of the Gospel is not given any significance, then this is no interpretation of the Gospel of John. He "knows Jesus only in his resurrected existence" (Luise Schottroff, see below). Jesus' compassion for the suffering is, then, deleted.

Günther Bornkamm, three articles in vol. 1 of his *Geschichte und Glaube [History and Faith]* (2 vols.; Munich: Kaiser, 1968, 1971):

a) "Zur Interpretation des Johannes-Evangeliums" ["On Interpreting the Gospel of John"], 104–21.

b) "Der Paraklet im Johannes-Evangelium" ["The Paraclete in the Gospel of John"], 68–89.

c) "Die eucharistische Rede im Johannes-Evangelium" ["The Eucharistic Discourse in the Gospel of John"], 60–67.

I concur with Bornkamm's rejection of Käsemann's hypothesis that Johannine Christology is a "naive docetism" (p. 117) and with his critique of Käsemann's biased interpretation of John 1:14.

If Bornkamm accords a high degree of significance to the farewell discourses in the first of these essays, this significance also must extend to that from which Jesus makes his farewell, namely, his speaking and working *before* the farewell. Yet it is precisely the meaning of this that Bornkamm seeks to limit as much as possible. Why? The assertion cannot be true that Jesus' farewell was faith's real hour of birth (p. 113). The man born blind, whom Jesus healed, believed in him. More important still is a fixed idiom that pervades the entire Gospel: the effects of Jesus' words and deeds during his journey. Throughout the Gospel, faith *in*

Jesus and turning *from him* is decided by the deeds and words of the Jesus who wandered and ministered upon the earth. The assertion that his farewell was faith's real hour of birth contradicts the facts. Why does Bornkamm conceal the substantial group of texts that express the opposite? The only thing he can have in mind is that before the cross and the resurrection there was no real faith as such; but then he should have stated this explicitly. In his view and in that of many others, only Jesus' death and resurrection are necessary for salvation, which he labels "the fruit of his death" (p. 113). Only faith in the cross and the resurrection is real faith, in this case. But where does the Gospel of John say this?

If it is only the post-Easter community that knows what faith means (p. 114), the statement in John 1:14 is not relevant; for it would be grotesque if Jesus had indeed done his works in many people, and if this is described by saying, "and he revealed his glory," but those who received these works did not know their meaning! Severing Jesus' death and resurrection from his ministry in life comes close to Paul's saying: "I do not know Christ according to the flesh" (2 Cor. 5:16).

Bornkamm (p. 117) does indeed state, "As far as . . . the aspect of Jesus' salvific significance is concerned, the evangelist . . . did not need to relinquish the earthly one but could . . . describe the history of Jesus afresh." This statement, however, gives the impression that "the earthly one" actually has no meaning for salvation. This is to misjudge the Gospel, which *as such* is an account of Jesus' history. To "relinquish the earthly one" would be tantamount to devaluing the Gospel.

Bornkamm is correct in saying that for the Gospel of John Gnosticism is presuppositional; such typically gnostic phrases as "you are from below, I am from above" cannot be explained any other way. Yet Bornkamm's explanation that "even the indisputably gnostic features in the Gospel" are meant to be understood differently is merely an assertion. They represent gnostic elements that, in part, stand in stark contradiction with the Gospel. They form an alien element within it, which can clearly be discerned in a later layer of the controversy dialogues between Jesus and the Jews in chs. 5–10. They have been added to, or inserted into, the history of Jesus, in about the same way as the controversy dialogues of Job's friends were inserted into the history of Job.

Yet we agree with G. Bornkamm in rejecting Käsemann's (and then Schottroff's) interpretation, in which the Gospel of John as a whole is given a gnostic explanation.

Luise Schottroff, *Der Glaubende und die feindliche Welt: Beobachtungen zum gnostischen Dualismus und seine Bedeutung für Paulus und das Johannesevangelium [The Believer and the Hostile World: Observations on Gnostic Dualism and its Significance for Paul and the Gospel of John]* (Neukirchen-Vluyn: Neukirchener, 1970), ch. 6: "Die Johanneische Gnosis" ["Johannine Gnosticism"], 228–296.

Johannine dualism, pp. 228–245. "The Johannine antitheses set salvation and disaster against each other as determiners of the essence of human beings and mythical figures" (p. 228). Thinking of these determiners of essence (is German Idealism's concept of "essence" intended here?), in terms of a time scheme, it is "inappropriate." The "expressions of essence" are "orientated to passage from their antithesis . . . , but are not to be construed as events within a passage of time" (p. 229).

The Gospel of John, however, speaks of a history, of a course of time that leads from the beginning of Jesus' ministry to its end. According to Schottroff, this presentation of a sequence of time is inappropriate. Hence, she also deems it irrelevant that the structure of the temporal sequence is marked with conspicuous clarity by travel references describing Jesus' path from the beginning to the end of his ministry. The travel references are supplemented with time references, especially those referring to the festivals. The extent of time is underscored by the references to the hour that had not yet come at the outset (in ch. 2) but then came with Jesus' suffering, death, and resurrection.

If in its temporal scope the history of Jesus of Nazareth is irrelevant for the author, she has modified the Gospel of John from the start. She speaks of a thought construct, the essence of which she is examining, but not of the history of Jesus of Nazareth.

The reason for this is evident at first sight. The antitheses that form the starting point for Schottroff are a characteristic motif in Gnosticism. These antitheses are timeless; the thinking they express is ahistorical. To this extent she is right. The author begins with this correctly perceived distinctive mark of Gnosticism and then endeavors to explain the entire Gospel of John from gnostic motifs. The fact that it gives an account of a history, as shown above, thus has to be dismissed as irrelevant. It follows from this first step that every event in the Gospel is transposed into timeless existence, into what the author calls "intrinsic."

Schottroff, then, must so interpret even the prologue that it is robbed of its character as an event: "In the beginning" for her is "not a reference to time but an intrinsic designation" (p. 232). The statement about creation in 1:3 is interpreted as an offer of salvation in 1:4: John interprets creation existentially (p. 233). The author has particular difficulties with 1:14; this is evident just from the observation that she must refer back to it repeatedly. Against all interpreters known to me, she insists that 1:14 is a gnostic statement.

The meaning of the visibility of the semeia, pp. 245–268. According to Schottroff, the miracle authenticates the miracle worker; it is meant to awaken faith in Jesus' miraculous power. The demand for a sign may be right and wrong. The right sign is not the miracle but the heavenly reality of the revealer (as frequently elsewhere, so here, too, a process is modified into being). The wrong sign relates to that which is within the world. John 4:46–53 may be used as an example. The miracle story is adopted as such, though in keeping with dualistic thought it is reinterpreted in terms of two realities. (The German term for "reality" [*Wirklichkeit*] has no plural form.) Jesus is seen correctly only if he is understood as a nonworldly revealer: "Jesus does indeed provide the regaining of physical health, but this is not the crucial issue" (p. 264). Jesus does indeed heal a person, but the healing is not the issue! The suffering of people and people themselves are not what Schottroff is thinking about. The dialogues in connection with the healings are not even mentioned. Yet without them the healings in the Gospel of John are incomprehensible. Indeed, this is precisely what makes the Gospel of John distinctive over against the Synoptics! If the healing-related dialogues are not even mentioned, the reason must be sought in this interpretation. In this case, the signs are mere abstractions. They have nothing to do with living human beings; people are puppets.

The origin of Jesus and the incarnation, pp. 268–283. For John, the origin of Jesus is something entirely commonplace. Alongside this there are statements about his heavenly origin. Both are true (one would like to know how). Following the categories of faith, the believer has both "kinds" of eyes(!) at his disposal, heavenly as well as earthly ones. Only the heavenly eyes remain relevant for him, no longer the physical ones. This indicates that in the gnostic view of humanity the human being is not a creature, for if physical existence is no longer relevant for him—not even the physical face—he does not perceive himself as creature. God did not create him with four eyes. Gnostic dualism divides the person into two beings, a believing and a physical being—hostile to one another—just as the world is divided into a heavenly and an earthly world. God's caring for the world (John 3:16), in the view of the author, John means the charge against, and the rejection of, the world; this highlights the decisive character of both faith and unbelief (p. 289). According to this interpretation, John even in 3:16 did not leave the premise of Gnosticism. This reinterpretation of a simple statement such as this is so contorted that no one to date has voiced agreement with it.

Like the human being and the world, so the revealer is a divided being. While John 1:14 indeed states that Jesus existed within this world, his essential being is not touched by it (so also Käsemann), for it is glory. John 1:14 has to be understood in terms of gnostic dualism (Bultmann, Schnackenburg, and Bauer hold otherwise). This once again demonstrates the basic premise of this interpretation: 1:14 depicts an event; for Schottroff, it speaks of being; she dismisses the event as irrelevant.

Concluding considerations, pp. 289–296. For John, Jesus is the revelatory figure of Gnosticism. He depicts him exclusively with reference to gnostic dualism: The world is "only a world in its hatred against God." A world created by God does not exist. The world that exists only in hatred against God is merely imaginary. Accordingly, the revealer is merely an imaginary revealer in gnostic dualism. For instance, Jesus is not, as the Gospel frequently says, sent into this world by God; this is merely a disguise. The "Son" is a nonworldly, heavenly figure; he is God walking upon the earth. This gnostic interpretation is not conversant with Jesus of Nazareth, even though it adopts a number of things from the Synoptic Gospels.

The reason for this is what was mentioned at the beginning: This interpretation ignores the fact that the Gospel of John recounts a history. The author repeatedly refers to "themes," as if the Gospel of John were an intellectually structured tractate, for example, on

p. 272. Everything transpiring on the stations of Jesus' journey, from the beginning to the end of his ministry, is irrelevant for Schottroff. The people with whom Jesus converses and among whom he works are merely imagined. It is not important that Jesus helps people and delivers them from their suffering.

What is particularly indicative is that a very significant component of the Gospel, Jesus' conversations with individuals, does not appear in Schottroff's interpretation at all. What happens on Jesus' journey in the Gospel is, to a large extent, dialogical event. If this is ignored, the Gospel of John cannot be understood. The author does not let the Gospel finish speaking for itself. In her interpretations, she always interrupts.

We concur with the author that the Gospel of John contains a whole series of clearly gnostic motifs, which she delineates in the first part of her book (contra H. Thyen). What is wrong is to allow these to define the Gospel of John as a whole. They are limited to a part of the controversy dialogues, more specifically the later layer. The fact that they define only part of the Gospel of John is confirmed, rather than refuted, in this study's forced attempt to subject the entire Gospel to a gnostic interpretation.

The most important criterion in distinguishing between gnostic and non-gnostic parts is their relationship to the Old Testament (see above, pp. 68–70).

Klaus Wengst, *Bedrängte Gemeinde und verherrlichter Christus: der historische Ort des Johannesevangelium als Schlüssel zu seiner Interpretation [Troubled Community and Glorified Christ: The Historical Place of the Gospel of John as a Key to its Interpretation.]* (2d ed.; Neukirchen-Vluyn: Neukirchener, 1981).

In the first, most extensive, part Wengst deals with introductory matters. His hypothesis is that the Gospel of John originated in Syria, in the southern part of the realm of King Agrippa II, in the context of small Christian communities troubled by Jews, in whose sphere of influence they lived. It is conceivable that the Gospel originated in Syria, but the specific time is subject to question. For one thing, the enemies of the believers are presumably identified simply as "Jews," and this is not a historical identification; for another, there is no certainty about whether the Gospel as a whole originated at one time, as Wengst assumes.

In his brief sketch of the history of research, Wengst points out the contrast between Bultmann and Käsemann: Concerning 1:14, Bultmann emphasizes the first part of the statement, while Käsemann emphasizes the second part. This is possible, however, only because both construe the statement as a description of essence, rather than as an event. Yet if it is construed as an event, which is without doubt the case grammatically, then both parts of the statement are equally important. Wengst rejects both viewpoints. In one decisive aspect, however, he correctly agrees with Bultmann, against Käsemann, that the Gospel of John construes Jesus as a real human being, rather than as God who walks upon the earth.

Wengst emphasizes that the Gospel narrates (better: gives an account of) the history of Jesus of Nazareth. But this does not fit with the fact that Wengst then addresses individual themes, such as expressions of sovereignty, Jesus as sovereign over his fate, the significance of Jesus' death. A narrative (i.e., an account) does not deal with themes; it is more important to inquire into its structure and parts. One of his themes is "the fate of the disciples." But it deals with the disciples only in the context of Jesus' death. He does not even mention that the largest part of what the Gospel says about the disciples deals with them in the context of Jesus' lifetime. Furthermore, the bulk of the Gospel, which speaks of Jesus' journey, of his deeds and words, becomes peripheral. It is not enough to select particular themes; the parts in their totality must be examined in their relationship to the whole. Wengst is not seriously concerned with the question whether the Gospel is a unit and how the many aporias, which render homogeneity very unlikely, are to be explained in the context of the Gospel as a whole. A mere collection of various themes cannot substantiate homogeneity.

Hartwig Thyen:

a) "Johannesevangelium" ["Gospel of John"], *Theologische Realenzyklopädie* (ed. G. Krause and G. Müller; 26 vols. to date; Berlin: de Gruyter, 1976–) 17.222–225.

b) "Ich bin das Licht der Welt: Das Ich- und Ich-Bin-Sagen Jesu im Johannesevangelium" ["I am the Light of the World: the I- and I-am Sayings of Jesus in the Gospel of John"], in *Jahrbuch für Antike und Christentum* 35 (1993) 1–26.

c) (with Detlef Puttkammer) *"Seht, euer Gott: Sieben Auslegungen zu Passionstexten aus dem Johannesevangelium"* (Behold your God: Seven expositions on passion texts in the Gospel of John), 1988 (=Texte zur Bibel 4, Arbeitsheft zur Bibelwoche 1988/89, 1988).

Two things stand out for me in the essays of H. Thyen:

1. In his essays, he emphasizes repeatedly that the Gospel of John is a literary piece, that is, it is meant to be read. He also describes it as Gospel, as the text indicates, but he does not state anywhere what the term *euangelion* means for him and how this term relates to that of literature. For him, the Gospel is significant as literature, not as Gospel.

2. Thyen emphatically points to the concluding verse of 20:31: "these are written that you may believe that Jesus is the Christ." How is a work to arouse faith when it is a literary piece and hence is meant for *reading* and

when it is often claimed that it is fictitious. The reader's attention is drawn to the remarkable achievement of the author, often according to purely aesthetic perspectives. But what he says merely indicates the possibility that it was so. Yet if it grants no certainty, how is the book to arouse faith?

Thyen frequently describes the literary work as a narrative and stresses its alleged narratival character. This description does not apply to the Gospel of John (nor to the other three). Narratives are governed by their own laws; they have a clearly recognized structure, as can be observed in the Old Testament. There is no such structure in the Gospel of John, even though some parts of it are given a narratival arrangement. It is an account and is clearly recognized as such by the travel references and time references. An account is based on facts, on what happened. In this connection, the account has something in common with the term "Gospel," for the "good news" speaks of what happened. If the author had begun with the term "account," the term "Gospel" could have taken on meaning as well. The term "literature," however, meaning merely "written," as Thyen often stresses, is far too broad to express something specific about the Gospel.

The principle of synchronic interpretation. Thyen calls for "a strict focus on the synchronic level of the message handed down"; in other words, the evangelist wrote the Gospel, all of it, at the same time. None of the groups of texts has a prehistory, as he states explicitly about the I-am sayings. Hence, the evangelist must have invented them in the course of writing. Thyen contradicts this, however, when he states that these I-am sayings are predicated upon statements found in the Old Testament or in the Synoptics. Many of the texts he describes as "play material" (cf. b: pp. 14, 20, 26; c: p. 33). If the evangelist plays with them, they must have been around before him. Thyen can even admit that parts of the Gospel are based on older texts: "Rather, John here seems to consider the . . . Easter narrative of the earlier tradition" (c: p. 38). Clearly, a completely synchronic interpretation is an illusion.

Coherence and aporias, uniformity. In agreement with most interpreters, Thyen observes that the Gospel "does not seem . . . to arise from one casting" (a: p. 203). In his history of research, he spends pages listing the works on "aporias"; most of them relate to matters of context. He cites Bultmann's criteria: syntax, grammar, semantics, pragmatics. But according to Thyen, these have only limited significance. For him, the context (i.e., coherence) is not something that may or may not be found in the text; rather, for him it is a principle, a postulate. If the text is to be interpreted synchronically, it *must* be coherent throughout, in small and large units: "1:1–21:25 is a coherent literary text"—and it *must be* that! Concerning a small unit, he says about 11:2, "It was Mary who anointed the Lord with ointment." Yet the anointing is not reported until 12:1ff. Here too, according to Thyen, the coherence is not disturbed. He knows how to explain away the aporia by means of bizarre fantasy. Or take the bread discourse in ch. 6, which poses difficulties contextually. Yet Thyen has an explanation for this as well: "In the second part, the person of Jesus is torn apart into its component parts of bread and flesh" (b: p. 16f.). In the farewell discourses, where most interpreters find difficulties with coherence, Thyen knows what to do: The discourse, or part of it, concludes in 14:31; the action continues with Jesus' appeal: "Rise, let us go hence." But in 15:1ff. Jesus' discourse continues. This represents a disturbed context. Thyen has a simple explanation for this. For him, Jesus' appeal is not directed to the disciples; instead, 14:31 is a signal "to the reader, who is to 'rise' at this point" (a: p. 216; b: p. 22).

The Gospel of John and Gnosticism. This is one of the most difficult factors in interpretation, and the debate about it is far from over. Thyen does not see major difficulties on this issue. Since for him the Gospel as a whole is a unit and all of it originated at the same time, there can be no serious difficulty between statements of the evangelist and those of Gnosticism, between biblical and gnostic motifs. Where gnostic language is suspected, the evangelist makes use of it, according to Thyen, and integrates it into his language; sometimes the evangelist couches words of Jesus in gnostic language. One only need glance at the history of research, for instance, the contrasting interpretations of Bultmann, Käsemann, Schnackenburg, and Schottroff, to see that things are not quite this simple.

Thyen says correctly that all attempts at "understanding gnosis merely as a post-Christian and intra-Christian heresy" (a: p. 219) have failed. "It is to be taken seriously, if not as a pre-Christian competitor, then at least as a rival of a fledgling Christianity, alongside and outside the latter" (ibid.).

Concerning the much debated issue of a present and future eschatology he argues, "As a 'personalized' eschatology, the Johannine eschatology in itself cancels out the erroneous contrast between future and present" (a: p. 218). Thyen does not realize that he thereby formulates a typically gnostic statement.

Another feature of Gnosticism, the establishment of a contrast (generally described as dualism), is apparent in the answers Jesus proffers the Jews in the controversy dialogues. Some of these answers are so contrasted with the I-am sayings of Jesus that they are not compatible with the proclamation of Jesus as it is known from the I-am sayings. In the latter, the words of Jesus are consistently good news; they invite and promise.

Conversely, in the controversy dialogues, one encounters sayings of Jesus that are rejecting, excluding, and condemning, in keeping with the motif of establishing a contrast. Thus, for instance, the anti-Semitic expression "your father the devil"! It is not the same Jesus speaking in both instances.

A formal viewpoint needs to be brought to bear here. The controversy dialogues are an independent complex that has been added to—that is, integrated into—the Gospel at a later date. Jesus' responses are made up in it. "Jesus" is a code name here for believers, just as "the Jews" is for unbelievers.

The sayings of Jesus in the Fourth Gospel have different forms, but for Thyen this seems to be inconsequential for interpretation. If the I-am sayings, as individual sayings (logia), in the Synoptic Gospels are typical for the proclamation of Jesus, partly in sequences, partly individually, it seems reasonable to assume that they were handed down to the writer of the Gospel in this form, for he adopts them in the form handed down. In this case, it is possible that these sayings were spoken by Jesus of Nazareth. The same cannot be said about the sayings of Jesus in the controversy dialogues, whose form and content diverge. Perhaps the linguistic forms should not be ignored altogether after all. I fail to grasp how, in light of these contrasts in form and content, it is possible to speak of the uniformity of the Gospel as a whole.

Thyen is correct in saying that, "for the interpretation of the Gospel of John, only the Old Testament can be accorded unqualified priority over against other analogies" (b: p. 5; cf. a: p. 220). It is not sufficient to recognize agreements in many of the details. Rather, one needs to ask the comprehensive question whether the discussion about God is the same in both cases and whether the concept of humanity and of history is identical. This cannot be argued in such general terms if parts of the Gospel have important differences regarding the Old Testament. This applies, in the first place, to the concept of time and history. It is characteristic of Gnosticism that neither time nor history is essential. Thyen argues for the unity of ch. 6. But besides the simple "I am the bread of life," which agrees entirely with the other I-am sayings, one encounters an interpretative discourse on the "bread from heaven," in which both the act of multiplying the loaves and the miracle of the manna in the wilderness are devalued and belittled. The complaint against both is that the multiplied loaves and the manna did not render immortal but the "bread from heaven" does. Two different voices are speaking here. It is impossible to affirm that the multiplication of the loaves is a sign authenticating Jesus and at the same time say that this had nothing to do with true bread. It is impossible to affirm the Old Testament and at the same say that the manna in the wilderness was not true bread. It is clear enough that the voice speaking here is gnostic because behind this statement is the denial of everything temporal, of every earthly gift. And it is sufficiently clear that the promise "if any one eats of this bread, he will live for ever" is gnostic: Only eternal life is real life. That 6:51b–56, the expansion of the bread motif with the flesh motif, is an addition is apparent even from the clumsy, hardly meaningful transition in v. 51b: "and the bread which I shall give . . . is my flesh."

The Gospel of John and dogmatics. From beginning to end, the Gospel of John is an account of an event. Like many others, Thyen has the urge to change what happens into what is, similar to Gnosticism. He says that the prologue deals with Jesus' divine being (a: p. 201). But the prologue has a verbal structure. It is concerned with an event: "The Word became flesh." If it is changed into nouns, it becomes more awkward and no longer expresses what the text is saying. In addition, in vv. 11–12, the prologue conveys the main parts of the Gospel (see above, pp. 4–5). The entire conception of the Gospel is formulated in these statements. Only when this is not noted can it be said, as Thyen does, that the farewell discourses are very much "up in the air" (a: p. 204). Verses 11–12 confirm that even the prologue has the structure of an account.

Thyen repeatedly moves from interpretation of an event to dogmatic language. What the Gospel reports about Jesus he turns into a Christology, a doctrine of Christ. Likewise there are "–ologies," eschatology and others, which occur frequently (though not as often as in Käsemann). Several times he states, "All Christology is messianology." The two terms are identical, however, except that one is Greek while the other is Hebrew. Or he states that John based eschatology on Christology; but John is not a dogmatic theologian.

Resurrection and eternal life (immortality). One of the most important differences between the Gospel of John and Gnosticism is that the latter prefers and stresses eternal life in terms of immortality. In Gnosticism the promise of eternal life occurs often, whereas the Gospel of John speaks of resurrection. Eternal life denotes being, a status: The believer has eternal life; death no longer affects him. The statement that "for believers death and judgment are already behind them" is gnostic. In contrast, the resurrection is an event presupposing and following death. The Gospel takes creatureliness seriously by recognizing the creature only within the boundaries of birth and death. *Every* person must die because he or she is a creature. Gnosticism does not acknowledge this limitation; the believer lives eternally. Abraham lives eternally. Jesus is preexistent; hence, the boundary of birth does not exist for him either. This is not the real, not the true Jesus whose parents are known.

"I am the resurrection and the life": this comparison arises from the story of the raising of Lazarus, as Thyen states appropriately. Yet he does not explain it on the basis of Lazarus rising but, on the basis of 5:19–29, where Lazarus is already being prepared (b: p. 22). Thyen thereby conceals the fact that John 5 speaks of immortality in gnostic language; in Jesus' sayings in ch. 11, however, resurrection and life belong together: "though he die, yet shall he live" (11:25), that is, the boundary of death is respected here.

The equation of Christ's exaltation in his death with his exaltation into the heavenly glory is also part of Gnosticism. This equation or merging of the two into one corresponds with gnostic timelessness. In the Synoptic Gospels, where Jesus' suffering and death are reported, Jesus' death and his resurrection are two distinct events that are separated in time; otherwise it would not be possible to give an account of them. The double entendre of exaltation can be only a gnostic interpretation.

Summary

Of the six interpretations, those of *Käsemann* and *Schottroff* are very similar, inasmuch as both consider the Gospel of John really a gnostic writing. For them, Jesus is not a historical figure but a disguised God or a divine being, a "God walking upon the earth." Jesus' earthly ministry, his words and his deeds, carry no meaning for them. Since gnostic thought is timeless and ahistorical, the same is also true for the Gospel of John; the "scheme of time" that it contains is inadequate. Gnostic dualism of "from below–from above," "earthly–heavenly" applies to the Gospel as well. One difference between the two is that *Käsemann* wraps the Gospel's Gnosticism in dogmatic language while *Schottroff* speaks of dualism from the perspective of "essence," in contrast to the earthly and heavenly reality in God, the world, and the human being.

Both outlines suffer from the same weakness. For both, the Gospel of John *must be* uniform because the gnostic character of the whole demands it. For this reason, neither of the two can admit to, that is, take into consideration, the enormous contrasts within the Gospel. In a different way, this weakness also applies to *Thyen,* who, since he regards the Gospel as literature of synchronic origin and hence as uniform, cannot acknowledge the contrasts in the Gospel.

Bornkamm is close to *Bultmann* in that both perceive Jesus as a human being. But *Bornkamm* does not argue that there is a fully (postulated) gnostic myth behind the Gospel, as *Bultmann* assumes. Another difference is that for *Bultmann* the Gospel of John as a whole arises from gnostic dualism. By contrast, *Bornkamm* states that the gnostic passages are different, and hence no longer "meant" in a gnostic sense in the fullest meaning of the term.

Peculiar to *Bultmann* is that he interprets the Gospel as the result of a redaction based on several sources. Peculiar to *Bornkamm* is that the hour when faith was born did not occur until Jesus' farewell, despite the fact that the Gospel often states that Jesus brought about faith in his earthly ministry.

H. Thyen is different from all those mentioned previously in that for him the Gospel of John is literature, designed to be read, and that the final form of its transmission (synchronic) is the one that is valid; there is no prehistory. He cannot, however, sustain the strictly synchronic understanding, because he argues that the Fourth Gospel, too, is predicated upon the Old Testament and presupposes the other three Gospels. He claims that it must be homogenous and assumes that he can explain all of the contextual disruptions. Since it is homogenous, there is no allowance for differences between statements of the Gospel and those of Gnosticism. The evangelist, he explains, sometimes couches Jesus' sayings in gnostic language. Yet he does not concede that they are often contrasted.

For *K. Wengst,* the emphasis is to identify the place and time of the Gospel's origin more precisely.

Even though these are only a few examples from the wealth of literature, they lead to the following conclusion: The two extremes—the Gospel of John as a gnostic writing and as a Christian writing in which gnostic elements are not meant in a gnostic sense—remain to be explained. Another remaining difficulty is that the serious theological contrasts within the Gospel cannot be explained adequately.

This calls for an inquiry into criteria that allow for these contrasts to be explained. At least *one* criterion is at hand in the question of how the gnostic and the non-gnostic motifs relate to the Old Testament.

Bibliographic References:

The most recent detailed compilation of the literature is found in H. Thyen's article in the *Theologische Realenzyklopädie,* 17.222–25.

A valuable collection of Gnostic writings can be found in James M. Robinson, ed., *The Nag Hammadi Library* (4th rev. ed., Leiden: Brill, 1996).

Scripture Index